Does God Exist?

Does God Exist?
A Dialogue

TODD C. MOODY

Hackett Publishing Company, Inc.
Indianapolis / Cambridge

04 03 02   2 3 4 5 6 7

For further information, please address

Hackett Publishing Company, Inc.
P.O. Box 44937
Indianapolis, Indiana 46244-0937

Library of Congress Cataloging-in-Publication Data

Moody, Todd C.
   Does God exist? a dialogue/Todd C. Moody.
       p.   cm.
   Includes bibliographical references.
   ISBN 0-87220-344-1 (cloth)   ISBN 0-87220-343-3 (pbk.)
   1. God. 2. God—Proof. 3. God—Proof—Controversial literature.
4. Theodicy. I. Title.
BT102.M615 1996
212′.1—dc20   96-25398
                                                              CIP

The paper used in this publication meets the minimum requirements
of American National Standard for Information Sciences—Permanence
of Paper for Printed Library Materials, ANSI Z39.48-1984.
                              ∞

Contents

Preface

Although it is widely believed that the word "dialogue" refers to something that is essentially contrasted to "monologue" (and dictionaries give some support to this view), it is important to remind ourselves that *dia* is the Greek preposition *through*, and that *logos* is about language and, more generally, discursive reasoning. A dialogue is a "talking through." It is a process of following an idea and offering resistance to it, seeing it as something that has an evolutionary character. That is, as we offer resistance to an idea, we discover whether it is strong enough to overcome that resistance, or, what is more likely, we learn how to make it stronger. In this age it may seem needlessly aggressive to apply the metaphor of strength to ideas, but I think it helps to keep in mind that there is something fundamentally oppositional or "agonistic" about this way of thinking. Even in natural evolution we think of "competition" among organisms; here the competition is among ideas. When we arrange this evolutionary process according to a conversational format, we get what we customarily think of as a "dialogue," and we also preserve the sense of commitment that the participants in the dialogue have; we understand that there is something at stake for them. This is one of the advantages of the dialogue form over straight philosophical prose.

The conversation of this book records a dialogue that has been taking place in my mind for about twelve years, with each idea in turn finding resistance there. As a teacher, I often wanted to engage my students in this dialogue in a manner that would allow them to see it as an unfolding process, not as a philosophical endpoint. So I composed a short dialogue and used it as a handout. During those twelve years my thinking took a number of twists and turns, and the dialogue got longer. As I pursued my reading and thinking, I continued to add to the dialogue, even when I was no longer using it in the classroom (because of a change in teaching assignments). It has now acquired a life of its own. David, Oscar, and Sophie, the interlocutors, are like old friends, and they too have grown and changed.

Most of the material here is very traditional, although there may be one or two unexpected points. The literature of philosophical theology is enormous, and I make no pretense that this treatment is comprehensive. Most of that literature, however, handles its conclusions as foregone; it is relentlessly partisan. Both the theist and the atheist seem often on the verge of concluding that those who disagree with them are somehow defective or deluded rather than simply mistaken. Indeed, this tendency is taken up in the final chapter of this book; the subject matter stimulates passionate discussion, so much so that it is often reserved for conversation among those of like mind, or even avoided altogether.

I have found that there are many who believe that it is somehow improper to engage in earnest discussion about a matter such as the existence of God. They say that nothing can be proved, and thus it's best to let people "believe what they want." While I can agree that no good purpose is served by one's trying to overpower another person in argument, I find it regrettable that anyone should back away from honest truth-seeking dialogue. Philosophy has a responsibility to keep such dialogue alive.

Therefore, what I have tried to do here is to preserve the passion and the fascination by allowing the arguments and ideas to follow their own lead. As a result, the logical flow is not as segmented and linear as it might have been if this were simply a monograph. There are digressions and switchbacks, often because unexpected resistance to an idea has been offered. That unexpected resistance is something that I have tried to preserve. But even though the interlocutors are partisans, they are also inquirers, and that is ultimately what keeps dialogue from dissolving into mere contest.

To preserve the natural flow of the dialogue, I have refrained from littering the text with such academic labels and terms as "ontological argument" when I could just as easily avoid them. Neither have I used a lot of citational gimmicks, like "as Aquinas said." Such details appear in the Suggested Readings essay at the end of the book. That is where the real participants in the dialogue are identified. As author, I don't mind being a pedant, but I don't want to force this role on my unwitting characters.

Chapters have to end somewhere, and I have had to make decisions about how much exploration of a particular question is "enough." This is by design a small book, and the reader should remember that my judgment as to how far to pursue a line of reasoning does not imply that one could not go much further. It is my hope that one will want to go much further indeed.

Chapter 1

The Burden of Proof

The scene is the game room at a college. It's late in the afternoon, and there are no students around except for three who have gathered around a battered pool table, taking turns in friendly games of eight-ball.

DAVID: Come on, God, just let me make this shot.

OSCAR: That's a fine way to talk. Does God go in for pool?

DAVID: Well of course it's just a figure of speech. I wouldn't really ask for God's help to win a game.

OSCAR: Seems to me that maybe you could use a little help. Are you serious, though? Do you really believe in God? I always thought you were reasonably intelligent. Not spectacularly intelligent, mind you, but—

DAVID: That's enough. Yes, it just so happens that I do believe, but I don't consider that my belief marks me as unintelligent. A lot of very intelligent people have believed in God, and there are many who still do.

OSCAR: Sure. A lot of intelligent people once believed in witchcraft, astrology, flat earth, and phlogiston, too. The point is, most of those people would reject such beliefs if they were around today and had access to the breadth of knowledge that we have.

DAVID: So your idea is that modern people who believe in God are unintelligent. Is that it?

OSCAR: Maybe "unintelligent" is a bit strong. Let's just say I think that, given our current state of knowledge, a belief in God is completely unsupported, even irrational. Is that better?

DAVID: Well, it's clearer. At least you're no longer calling theists idiots, and that must be a step in the right direction. Still, what makes you so sure that God doesn't exist? Hand me that chalk, will you?

OSCAR: Here. In the first place, no one has ever been able to prove that he does exist.

DAVID: But that doesn't prove that he doesn't.

OSCAR: Naturally. But the burden of proof is on the theist.

DAVID: Why? That sounds like a cheap debater's trick to me.

OSCAR: Not at all. The burden of proof isn't arbitrary. There are logical principles involved here. For one thing, if a person makes a claim that is on the face of it contrary to common sense, then it's that person's job to show that common sense is wrong. Nobody can see God, or hear him, or touch him, so common sense tells us that he isn't there. The burden of proof is on anyone who says he is.

DAVID: Hold on a minute. Aren't you leaning pretty hard on "common sense" here? It seems to me that it's a stretch to use common sense as a principle for discussing something like the existence of God. There are a lot of things that exist that we can't see or hear or touch. Numbers, for example. Does common sense tell you that they don't exist, either?

OSCAR: They *don't* exist in the way that you and I do. They're just ideas; they depend on us for existence. I don't doubt that the idea of God exists, any more than I doubt that the idea of Santa Claus exists. What I doubt is that either one of these ideas is about anything *real*.

SOPHIE: Pardon me for butting in, but there's something very interesting about what you just said, Oscar.

OSCAR: Thank you. I try to say interesting things. When I can't, I settle for true things.

SOPHIE: And when you run out of true things—but never mind. What you said was that numbers are ideas that depend on us for existence. Did you mean that to be interesting, or merely true?

OSCAR: It's both.

SOPHIE: Would you go further and say that anything that depends on numbers is also therefore dependent on our minds for its "reality," if I may use that word?

OSCAR: I'm not sure where you're going with this, but, sure, I'll accept that claim. What did you have in mind?

SOPHIE: Just this: Some truths depend on numbers, such as the truth of the statement that $2 + 2 = 4$. Since you are evidently an atheist, I take it that you would say that before the evolution of life in the universe, there were no minds around at all.

OSCAR: I'm beginning to get the drift. Anyway, yes, before there was life, there were no minds. If there are any nonliving minds, such as those of robots, they would have to have been produced by living beings, and so they'd have come *after* them.

SOPHIE: Then this commits you to the very interesting claim that before life evolved it was not true that 2 + 2 = 4.

OSCAR: Okay, but it wasn't false either.

SOPHIE: I hope you don't think it's any less startling to say that at some point in the past it was neither true nor false that 2 + 2 = 4.

OSCAR: What does it really mean to say that a truth "exists," anyway? Is it the same as saying that something is true? It might make sense to say that before there was life it was true that 2 + 2 = 4, but this thing that we're calling "the truth that 2 + 2 = 4" didn't exist until later. It depends on what you mean by a "truth," right? If it's something like a true *belief*, then I have no trouble saying that mathematical truths didn't exist until there was somebody to believe them. But what does all this have to do with God, anyway? I thought God was supposed to be *more* than an abstraction and more than a belief.

DAVID: Well, you started it, with your "burden of proof" jive.

SOPHIE: You don't get off the hook that easily, David. There's another argument that puts the burden of proof right back in your lap. In claiming that God exists, you're making an *existence claim*, and I think it's a different kind of existence claim from the claim that things like numbers exist. Oscar is right to reject the analogy. When you're discussing whether something exists, you can claim either that it does or it doesn't, or that you don't know whether it exists or not. It makes sense to me that the person who claims that something does exist is the one who has the burden of proof.

DAVID: Why? If the theist can't prove that God does exist, and no one can prove that he doesn't, why not just leave it in the "unknown" category? I'm not saying that a good case can't be made for God's existence, but I don't see why the atheist shouldn't also have to make a strong case. Why should atheism be the "default" position, with the atheist being left off the hook?

SOPHIE: Maybe this is the "common sense" part. How do you decide what to believe in, in general?

DAVID: I don't understand your question.

Sophie: I mean, do you usually believe only in the things that you have good reason to believe in, or do you believe in everything that hasn't been shown *not* to exist?

David: Aren't they just about the same thing?

Sophie: No. Think about it. Do you believe there are unicorns?

David: No.

Sophie: Why not?

David: They're mythological creatures, inventions of the human imagination.

Sophie: But how do you know that?

David: I see. I guess I don't believe in unicorns because I've never been given any good reason to believe in them. No one has ever found one, or the remains of one, or anything like that.

Sophie: Right. You have a choice. You can say, "I won't believe in unicorns until I have conclusive evidence for their existence," or you can say, "I'll believe in unicorns until there is conclusive evidence that they don't exist." If you make a point of thinking the latter way, you'll end up believing that everything exists that hasn't been proven *not* to exist. Common sense says don't think like that, or you'll end up believing in a lot of nonexistent things.

David: What's wrong with keeping an open mind?

Sophie: There's nothing wrong with it, but you want to be careful about what it means to keep an open mind. The way I see it, open-mindedness means being willing to look at new evidence and to modify one's beliefs in the light of it. If there's no evidence *for* unicorns, I wouldn't call it open-mindedness to believe in them until it has been proven that there aren't any. That's just silly. On the other hand, if someone found what appeared to be the skeleton of a unicorn in a peat bog somewhere, then open-mindedness would mean taking the discovery seriously as evidence in favor of the existence of unicorns. It means being willing to revise your beliefs.

To be open-minded doesn't require that we be undecided, though. To insist that unicorn believers and unicorn disbelievers share the burden of proof equally means that everyone should be a "unicorn agnostic." But you can hardly ever prove that something does *not* exist; so common sense says you don't remain undecided while waiting for a nonexistence proof. How could you prove that there are no unicorns? You could say that no matter where you've looked, you haven't found one, and nobody else has found one either. It would still be possible that there is someplace where nobody has looked, and that's where the unicorns are. You've already said that you don't believe in unicorns, David. Are you a unicorn agnostic?

DAVID: No. It's a good point. I brought in the point about open-mindedness because I've met many people who gave the impression that nothing could ever get them to revise their disbelief in God, no matter how powerful the reasons might be. It fits what you're saying about open-mindedness to say that such people are not open-minded; their beliefs are not open to revision.

OSCAR: Are yours?

DAVID: I like to think so, Oscar. The fact that I haven't always believed in God proves it.

OSCAR: It only proves that you used to be open-minded, not that you still are.

SOPHIE: Fascinating as this is, I don't think I want to get into a discussion of who is open-minded and who isn't. Let's just agree that sound reasoning on either side of the question ought to make a difference to an open-minded person, and then get on with it.

DAVID: That's fine with me, since I think there is good evidence for God's existence.

OSCAR: I can't wait to see what this evidence is, my friend. It's your shot, as we say in billiards.

During a lull in the discussion, David wins the game. Sophie steps up to the table and racks the balls. She then takes Oscar's cue stick and waits for David to break.

Sophie: Nice break, David. I won't comment about who may or may not be on your side.

DAVID: Thank you. You know, even though I can see the point of the burden of proof's being on the theist, there's still something odd about the very idea of a "proof" of something like God's existence.

SOPHIE: What's strange about it?

DAVID: I'm not sure how to put it, but it has to do with what you were saying before, about existence claims. Usually, you don't use arguments to prove that a thing exists; you just produce it, or point to it—you show that it's out there. Arguments are only verbal, and usually when we want to show that something exists we do more than just talk about it. But when it comes to God, producing or showing or pointing is out of the question, in a literal sense at least.

OSCAR: Hah! And what does that tell you?

SOPHIE: Wait a minute, Oscar. Let's not jump to any conclusions. Can you give an example of what you're talking about, David?

DAVID: Sure. If you asked me whether green roses exist, the best thing for me to do would be either actually to show you one, or to offer some evidence, such as a picture, that you would accept. Proving that something exists is usually some form of *showing*.

SOPHIE: What about a proof that a prime number greater than any given number exists? Would that involve showing?

DAVID: There we go again. I had a feeling you would think of something like that. The trouble is, I don't really want to defend the view that God is an abstraction, like a prime number. Oscar made the point that when we talk about the existence of numbers we're talking about a different kind of existence, so it could involve a different kind of showing. In fact, mathematicians do use something like "showing"; it's called "constructive proof." In a constructive proof, you show *how* you can produce a prime number greater than a particular given number. But I really don't think God is a mathematical object, or even much like one.

SOPHIE: The problem, then, is that there are two kinds of proof, depending on the kind of thing it is whose existence you're trying to prove. If it's a concrete object, the proof is in the showing; if it's an idea or abstraction, the proof is purely formal, like a proof in geometry or logic. Is that about right?

DAVID: That's it exactly. And the real problem is that neither kind of proof is appropriate. It's as if our usual conceptions of evidence just don't apply in this particular case.

OSCAR: This sounds like an evasion to me. Besides, it amounts to saying that a convincing case for the existence of God just can't be made, which is what I would say anyway. And that's the same as saying that there's no good reason to believe in God.

SOPHIE: It may turn out that way, but I think you've both overlooked a third kind of proof, one that applies to nonabstract things but is not just a kind of showing.

DAVID: That's good news. What kind of proof did you have in mind?

SOPHIE: The basic idea is this: Suppose you're a detective at the scene of a crime. You look at the physical evidence and say, "There must have been an accomplice. The criminal could not have done this alone." In a sense you've proved the existence of an accomplice (assuming that your reasoning is sound) without actually producing him. This sort of proof is used all the time in science. By looking at masses and charges, physicists were able to deduce that there must be a particle that has no charge but that is approximately equal in mass to the proton: the neutron. In biology, Mendel showed that inheritance of traits follows mathematical patterns; it therefore made good sense to suppose that there must be some substance in the cell that carries genetic information: DNA. That last example is especially good, since the showing—the actual discovery that DNA was "the right stuff" for this job—didn't come until much later. The main focus of this sort of proof is, given what clearly *is* the case, to show that something else *must be* the case. This approach ought to be suitable for proving the existence of God, if you can actually get the proof to work.

DAVID: You're right, Sophie. Apparently those philosophy courses are not a complete waste of time, after all.

OSCAR: *Now* who's jumping to conclusions? If I'm not mistaken, this sort of reasoning was also used to demonstrate the existence of phlogiston, caloric fluid, astrology, and a lot of other bull—

SOPHIE: Now that's hardly a fair objection, Oscar. Just because a logical method has been misapplied—as it might have been by astrologers, for all I know—it doesn't follow that it *never* works. And you shouldn't put phlogiston and astrology in the same category. The theory of phlogiston was a reasonable one, given the state of knowledge at the time. After all, when you burn a heavy log, you end up with a fairly light pile of ashes. It's not unreasonable to suppose that something that was in the log was liberated during the burning. In fact, that *is* what happens, but now we know that what is liberated is not phlogiston. This only shows that the kind of reasoning we're talking about is not infallible. But there have been faulty mathematical proofs, too. Is it then the proper response to trash the whole notion of mathematical proof?

DAVID: She's right, Oscar. The trick at this point is to put together a good proof—or at least a good argument, and that doesn't require infallibility.

OSCAR: Okay, okay. Even so, these arguments are always a bit risky, aren't they? There's a real difference between them and mathematical proofs. In mathematics, if you come up with a proof that contradicts something else that you've already proved, then you really have "misapplied" the method of mathematical proof, as Sophie put it. With the kind of arguments Sophie is talking about, you could do everything right and still end up being completely wrong.

DAVID: How is that, Oscar?

OSCAR: Easy. It's always possible that information is missing that would lead you to a different conclusion. When the detective says "There must have been an accomplice," he's basing his reasoning on the information he has at the time. But there could be other information that he doesn't have yet that would be relevant. Thus it would not be a case of his "misapplying" the method, but proof of this sort is only as good as the completeness and accuracy of the information on which it is based.

SOPHIE: You're right, Oscar, but that's just the way it is when we step outside of domains like mathematics where we can severely restrict the conditions of relevance and get into definitions, axioms, and rules. The best David can hope for is a case for God's existence that is consistent with our best understanding about the universe. That understanding may not be good enough, but we're stuck with it.

OSCAR: Well, as far as I can see, the burden hasn't shifted. So let's hear what you can come up with, David.

DAVID: I'm willing to try, but it occurred to me that it's really not true that, despite Sophie's persuasive argument about unicorns, it is never reasonable to try to prove that something does *not* exist.

OSCAR: So now you want me to prove that God doesn't exist? How am I supposed to do that?

DAVID: One way to prove that a thing doesn't exist is to prove that it *couldn't* exist. If you can prove that, then you don't have to go around looking for the thing at all. So the atheist isn't completely out from under the burden of proof.

SOPHIE: I don't agree, David. Remember, the burden of proof can't be *shared*. To say that one side has the burden of proof is to say that the other side's position is acceptable unless proven wrong. It makes no sense to say that about both sides. I think we've already seen why the burden of proof is on the theist, and the fact that the atheist might also be able to prove his or her case doesn't change that. Of course, if the atheist can prove that God doesn't exist, then it doesn't matter that he or she didn't have the burden of proof to start with.

Another point is that atheists might not agree among themselves that God couldn't exist, even though they agree that he doesn't. Therefore, the atheist can't be *required* to prove that God couldn't exist. It's not part of the atheist's "creed." Maybe we could distinguish between "strong atheism"—the belief that it's impossible for God to exist—and "moderate atheism"—the belief that God could exist but doesn't.

OSCAR: Is there a "weak atheism"?

SOPHIE: I'm thinking that this would be the ground occupied by the agnostic, who says that we are not in a position to know whether God exists. To some theists this is indeed a form of atheism, but some atheists find it too—well—weak.

DAVID: So which kind of atheist are you, Oscar?

OSCAR: I'm not an agnostic. I think agnosticism is a cop-out. That is, I think that the very admission that we are not in a position to know that God exists is a good argument for the case that he doesn't. After all, I'm not an agnostic about unicorns, as Sophie was saying earlier. I think the whole burden-of-proof question puts agnosticism off the map. As for whether I'm a strong or a moderate atheist, I'll have to think about that. Meanwhile, I'll see what you have to say.

Chapter 2

The First Cause

Sophie, having won the second game, suggests that they go for coffee. As they cross the campus, the discussion continues.

DAVID: I guess my strongest instinct about these things is that the universe had to come from somewhere. I've heard about the scientific theories. The Big Bang theory, for example, is the claim that everything in the universe was once concentrated in some tiny space. There was a tremendous explosion. Supposedly we are in the midst of that explosion—or its aftermath. I can't really judge that theory on its scientific merits, but apparently there is good evidence to support it. However, the theory doesn't really account for that original ball of stuff; so the problem of the origin of the universe is just pushed back to *before* the Big Bang. That's where I think you have to bring God into the picture. The great thing about this view is that it shows that there needn't be any real conflict between science and religion.

OSCAR: That's all very moving, but it isn't very convincing. For one thing, even if one grants that the argument proves the existence of a god—which I don't—it doesn't prove that that god still exists. Maybe he was destroyed in the explosion. Furthermore, it doesn't prove that he is a good god, even if he does still exist. And it doesn't prove—

SOPHIE: Hold it; back off. I think it's fair to let David prove one thing at a time. It's ridiculous to expect one argument to prove *everything* about God. If you have a criticism, you should direct it at the argument, not at the absence of further arguments for other conclusions.

OSCAR: All right. I was just making a point. As a matter of fact, I don't think the argument can stand on its own anyway. Let me paraphrase it. "Everything has to come from somewhere. The universe is something. So it had to come from somewhere, and that's what we call God." Is that a fair gloss on your argument, David?

DAVID: Yes, that sums it up.

OSCAR: Well, it's illogical. If everything has to come from somewhere, and God exists, then God is something, too. That would mean that God had to come from somewhere. Where?

DAVID: God is eternal. He has always existed. There is no time before which God did not exist. Therefore, he didn't "come from" anywhere.

OSCAR: I thought you'd say that. What you've done is to make an exception to your first premise, that everything has to come from somewhere. What you're really saying is that everything has to come from somewhere, *except for eternal things*. The refutation of your argument is obvious. If you can make an exception for God, why not just make an exception for the universe itself and drop the "God hypothesis" as unnecessary? Why not just say that there is no time before which the universe didn't exist? It's as easy to postulate that the universe is eternal as it is that God is.

DAVID: That wouldn't explain, well, creation. I mean, the idea is that the universe had to be created, and that's why there must be a God. If you say that the universe is eternal, you're saying that it wasn't created at all; it just *is*.

OSCAR: Fine. If creation means an event that resulted in a universe coming into existence, and there wasn't previously a universe—and I don't know what else you might mean by "creation"—then there's no compelling reason to believe that creation ever happened. It's perfectly consistent to say that the universe has just always been there. In fact, it's very strange that you insist that the universe "had to be created," as if creation were something that you were in the habit of observing. Maybe "creation" in the sense that you're using the word is just nonsense. I mean, you're talking about creation of something from nothing, not just rearranging what was already there. Is there any evidence that this sort of thing ever occurred?

DAVID: You're right to say that I don't mean creation as a kind of rearrangement of materials, like creating a castle out of sand.

OSCAR: Exactly. You don't want to say that God created the universe out of some *ingredients*. You want to say that he created it out of nothing at all, by an act of will, somehow—right?

DAVID: Yes.

OSCAR: What a concept. So, if there was no universe before God created it, *where was he?* If God existed at all, didn't there have to be someplace for him to exist in? And if there was such a place, even if there was nothing in it but God, then wasn't there already a universe?

DAVID: I'm not going to pretend that I know the answers to those questions, Oscar. Still, I think it's at least conceivable that God exists outside of space, if you can make sense of that, and that he created space and everything in it.

OSCAR: Outside of space? I'm afraid I don't follow you. If God exists, doesn't he have to exist *somewhere?*

SOPHIE: I can think of a lot of things to say about that, Oscar. Think of something like the earth's gravity. I believe you'd say it's real enough, but does it exist in some specific place? And what about your thoughts—do they occupy space?

OSCAR: Maybe gravity exists everywhere, but that's easier to understand than something that exists nowhere. As for my thoughts, as far as I'm concerned they take place right here in my head.

SOPHIE: You may have a *theory* about your thoughts according to which they take place in your head, but it seems to me that there's nothing about your thoughts themselves that places them in your head or anywhere else. You don't actually experience them as having a location in space.

OSCAR: Sure I do. My thoughts are right in here, in this internal space from which I can look out through my eyes onto the external world. What's so mysterious about that?

SOPHIE: You've been seduced by your own spatial metaphors, for that's all they are. Keep in mind that everything in your head, every neuron and blood vessel, is part of what you are calling the "external world." To say that your thoughts are "internal" in some sense and the rest of the world is somehow "external" to them may be a useful metaphor, but it doesn't carry any literal meaning. If thought is an important aspect of God's nature, we are not required to posit an external world in which to locate it, that's all.

OSCAR: I think we're getting sidetracked—

SOPHIE: Arguments don't always go in straight lines.

OSCAR: I'm willing to leave open the question of where God

was before he created the universe. But nothing requires me to believe in such a concept as creation.

DAVID: I see your point now. I guess anyone who doesn't share the intuition that the universe had to be created would not be impressed by the argument I gave.

OSCAR: Right. Anyone who does share that intuition wouldn't need an argument. You're stating *as a premise* that the universe had to be created, and then concluding that God created it. But your argument should start with premises that the theist and skeptic can agree on, or else there's no point in making it. As a skeptic, I have trouble with the very idea of creation, so you'll have to find some other premise to work with.

DAVID: You're right, Oscar. Maybe the problem is that it's too vague to say that the universe had to "come from" somewhere. It would be better to say that since everything that happens has a cause, that implies some first cause, to get things started.

OSCAR: That is at least clearer, David. It's also more clearly defective. The same counterargument applies. If you're going to say that God is the first cause, you're making an exception to the premise that everything has a cause. And there's no logical difficulty in saying that the chain of cause and effect extends back infinitely into the past, without a beginning.

DAVID: Isn't there? If time extends back infinitely into the past, then an infinite amount of time had to elapse before the present moment could occur. But that seems impossible. If we had to wait an eternity before getting to now, then now would never get here.

SOPHIE: That's an interesting argument, David, but I'm not sure that it works the way you think. There doesn't seem to be any logical objection to saying that the future is infinite. It doesn't mean, however, that there is some future event that is infinitely far away from the present in time. Every event, no matter how far in the future, is only a finite amount of time away from the present. As I see it, the same principle applies to the past. Even if the past is infinite, every moment of the past is still only finitely removed in time from the present. There is no moment, in the past or future, that is *not* finitely removed in time from the present, regardless of whether the past and future are finite or infinite.

DAVID: So does that refute the first-cause argument?

SOPHIE: Not so fast. There's another way of looking at it. It's logically consistent to say that God is the cause of all subsequent effects *and* that God is self-caused. If you state it that way, you haven't made an exception to the premise that "everything has a cause."

DAVID: That's right, Oscar. It's just as consistent as your statement that the universe has always existed, but it has the further advantage of capturing the intuition that the universe had to be created.

OSCAR: It may be consistent, but that doesn't persuade me to believe in it. I'll need more than consistency for that. As for your intuition that the universe had to be created, that's not *my* intuition. What you're telling me is that this argument is reducible to an appeal to intuition. To you it's intuitive that the universe was created; to me it isn't. The fact that the idea of a self-caused being is more hospitable to your intuition is no reason for *me* to believe it. Furthermore, I think there is something very counterintuitive about the notion of anything's being "self-caused." At the very least, it's a very alien idea. Can we point to any examples of that sort of thing in nature?

DAVID: No, but it isn't fair to limit God to the same principles that apply to natural processes. After all, he's supposed to be the author of those principles.

OSCAR: Once again, you're assuming what you're supposed to be proving. You're saying that God is the author of the laws of nature and therefore not bound by them. I don't believe that God exists, and you're supposed to be trying to convince me that he does. You can hardly expect that sort of a move to have any logical force.

DAVID: I don't think I'm unreasonable in saying that if God is the *author* of the laws of nature, then he is not necessarily bound by them. What's wrong with that?

OSCAR: I'm saying that the notion of something causing itself runs completely counter to everything we know about nature. I'm not even sure it makes sense. After all, don't causes come *before* their effects? Wouldn't that mean that God, in order to be the cause of himself, had to exist before he existed? A proof should start with premises that both parties to the argument can accept. You can hardly expect me to accept this crazy stuff.

SOPHIE: That's a reasonable point, Oscar. It is important to find premises acceptable to both sides. If you can find none, there's nothing to hang your argument on. Even if that happens, you've at least learned that the disagreement is *deep*, that it is at the level of basic principles. On the other hand, the fact that a self-caused being is something different from what we are used to in nature is not a fatal objection. If God actually created what we call nature, it makes sense that he would have properties that we would call, well, supernatural. Being self-caused could be an example of such a property.

Oscar: Supernatural? How about self-contradictory? My point is that self-causation doesn't even make sense. If you are going to say that God is so mysterious that even the laws of logic don't apply, then I have to exit this discussion right here, because that would mean that the theist can say pretty much anything, without worrying about whether it makes sense.

Sophie: No one's trying to abandon logic here. But let's look at the matter more closely. Are causes always prior to effects?

Oscar: That's how it looks to me.

Sophie: What about the tides? What causes the tide to rise and fall?

Oscar: The moon. That is, the moon's gravitational field.

Sophie: But does the moon *do something* prior to the tidal effects that produces them? Is this a case of a prior effect causing a later one?

Oscar: The moon had to be there first, before there could be any tides.

Sophie: Yes, but that's a bit misleading. To say that the moon had to "be there first" suggests that there was some event—the arrival of the moon—that initiated subsequent events, namely the tides. But it is more accurate to say that the moon's gravity is *continuously causing* the tides.

Oscar: Okay, I concede the point. How does this help to make sense of self-causation?

Sophie: It shows that there is a kind of causation that doesn't require that causes precede their effects, which means that self-causation, even if it is unusual, isn't self-contradictory.

David: It also allows us another way to think about creation. Instead of its having been a single event in which the whole natural world was launched into existence, we can think of God as *continuously creating* the natural order, sustaining the laws of nature by a continuous act of will.

OSCAR: I will admit that is a different way of thinking about God and creation. Still, your arguments seem to have moved slyly from evidence that God *does* exist to reasons why he *might* exist. Even if I grant the possibility that God *could* be a self-caused being, and that he might be continuously creating the universe, you're a long way from convincing me. The premise "Every event has a cause" may well be consistent with continuous creation, but it's also consistent with a beginningless, endless, and creationless sequence of causes and effects.

DAVID: I believe my argument has the advantage that it explains more. Your view leaves the whole world unexplained. Maybe some coffee will give me some better ideas.

SOPHIE: Maybe. You know, there's one other thing that bothers me about the first-cause argument. I'm not really sure I like the premise that everything has a cause.

OSCAR: Wow! Even I didn't have any trouble with that part.

SOPHIE: I know. But the worldview according to physics has changed a lot in the last fifty or so years. Apparently there are some events at the quantum level of reality, such as the spontaneous decay of a single atom of a heavy isotope, that are regarded as uncaused, purely random events.

OSCAR: I don't know anything about isotopes, but it sounds to me like a case of just not *knowing* the cause. That's different from saying that there isn't any cause.

SOPHIE: Yes, it's very different. The physicists are aware of the difference, and some of them still insist that these events are simply not caused.

OSCAR: So they haven't yet worked it out to everyone's satisfaction?

SOPHIE: That's right. At least they are still discussing the philosophical implications; they're pretty happy with the purely mathematical and scientific parts of the theory. The claim that every event has a cause is looking less and less self-evident. Physical theories are always changing, of course, but it seems fair to say that we can no longer take for granted the claim that every event has a cause. And in philosophy, people have been questioning the doctrine of universal causation—which is what philosophers call it—for centuries.

DAVID: I've read about quantum indeterminacy too, but I'm thinking that it might be a problem for the claim that everything has a cause in the sequential, cause-then-effect sense, but not in the continuous causation sense that we were just talking about.

SOPHIE: I think you've gone about as far with the first-cause argument as you can go. Oscar's not impressed. Maybe you should try a different approach.

Chapter 3

A Necessary Being

Coffees in hand, the three go to a table in a remote corner of the cafeteria. David is somewhat crestfallen by the apparent failure of his earlier arguments.

SOPHIE: So what's the next move, David?

OSCAR: Maybe it's your move, Sophie. You haven't really stuck your neck out yet. Which side are you on, anyway?

SOPHIE: I'm not sure that I'm on any side that I've heard so far. At least, I haven't heard a position that I would really go to bat for.

OSCAR: Typically evasive. You're just trying to dodge the issue, and that means you're probably a secret theist.

DAVID: Your turn on the rack, Sophie.

SOPHIE: Listen, you guys. I like to work things out in an orderly manner. David started out with a fairly straightforward argument for the existence of God. It may not have been entirely persuasive, but then I don't think we've really covered the terrain yet.

OSCAR: What's left to cover?

SOPHIE: Well, there's one famous attempt to prove the existence of God on purely logical grounds. Maybe you should hear about it.

DAVID: You'll have to do the talking, Sophie. I don't think I know anything about this one.

SOPHIE: The argument starts with a definition of God. The idea is that you can't really do much in the way of proving unless you have a precise conception of the entity whose existence you want to prove.

OSCAR: I would have said that myself, except I didn't really think that the pious would dare to define God.

SOPHIE: Maybe you'll like this definition: God is the most perfect conceivable being. Notice that this is much stronger than the statement that God is the most perfect actual being. It says that you can't even conceive of a more perfect being.

OSCAR: Okay, but what's "perfect"? That's a pretty vague term to use in a supposedly precise definition. Perfect according to whom?

SOPHIE: It's easier to approach it from the negative side. Imperfections are more understandable than perfections. An imperfection is any shortcoming, any way in which a thing fails to measure up to what it could conceivably be. For humans, mortality would be an example of an imperfection.

OSCAR: That implies that we could be immortal. Isn't that a pretty dubious proposition?

SOPHIE: It only implies that we could *conceivably* be immortal. We have some idea of what would count as immortality, and we know that we fall short of it. So that's an imperfection.

OSCAR: Okay. So God is the being with the fewest conceivable imperfections, is that it?

SOPHIE: Right. And that immediately tells you that God must have no imperfections, since if he had even one we would be able to conceive of a god who didn't have that particular imperfection. For God to be the most perfect conceivable being, he can have no imperfections at all.

OSCAR: Fine. I have no objection to that. In fact, it seems to make it even less likely that God exists. I think that I could always imagine a being more perfect than any given being. That would mean that no given being could be God.

SOPHIE: But here's the point. If a thing doesn't exist, that in itself is a kind of a defect, or shortcoming, as long as we could conceive of its existing. If the most perfect conceivable being didn't exist, we'd be able to conceive of a more perfect being, namely one who does exist. It follows that the most perfect conceivable being must actually exist.

OSCAR: Oh, come on now, Sophie. You're not serious about this one, are you? You seem to be saying that if we *define* God in the right way, then he just has to exist. Is that really the argument? Are you really claiming that God exists *by definition*?

SOPHIE: You could put it that way. I don't think it's any worse than saying that four-sided triangles or things that are black and white all over don't exist by definition. What it comes down to is this: Existence is essential to the very idea of an all-perfect being. And I think you should realize that this way of thinking about God is itself the result of a long process of evolution. This is a great step beyond just thinking of a God as mighty or fearsome.

OSCAR: I'm disappointed. The definition may be sophisticated, but this argument is a real abuse of logic. It's just the sort of thing that gives philosophy a bad name. Why, you just stick existence in there as if it were just one more property that a thing might have. You say that if a thing doesn't exist, that's an imperfection. That's just silly. If something is imperfect—without even getting into the question of whether you have really made the concept of perfection clear—then it's imperfect because of the properties it has. If it doesn't exist, it's not imperfect; it just doesn't have any properties at all.

SOPHIE: Can't a thing be imperfect because of the properties it *lacks?*

OSCAR: What do you mean?

SOPHIE: We think of blindness as an imperfection because a blind person lacks the property of being able to see.

OSCAR: That's a bit tricky, isn't it? A lot of things lack the property of being able to see: rocks, bicycles, peanut butter sandwiches—is it an imperfection for a rock to be "blind"? I think it makes more sense to say that imperfection exists when something has properties that it shouldn't have, or lacks properties that it should have. Lacking a property doesn't in itself make a thing imperfect.

SOPHIE: What about the idea that for God to lack existence would be an imperfection?

OSCAR: It's a bad idea. I can make sense of the idea that people should be able to see, that fish should be able to swim; but I can't make sense of the idea that God—or anything else—should exist. That's why I don't like thinking of existence as a property of a thing. If something exists, then it has properties, and we can talk about its imperfections; otherwise, forget it.

SOPHIE: Don't you think that when something ceases to exist, it loses something?

OSCAR: No, I don't. When something ceases to exist, it doesn't lose anything; it's just lost, gone. We lose *it.* When a person dies, for example, we say, speaking loosely, that he lost his life. That's okay, because we all understand that losing your life is not really like losing your shoe; it's just a manner of speaking. When you lose your shoe, you are still around to bear the loss. When you lose your life, you're not. What we call "losing your life" really means that you cease to exist. So you haven't lost anything, since you're not around to bear the loss. It's the rest of us who have lost you.

SOPHIE: So after I die I don't have the property of being dead?

OSCAR: That's right. You don't have any properties, because you're not there. I think that when we say "Sophie is dead," it's just a way of saying that the world no longer has Sophie in it. I definitely don't think it's a way of saying that Sophie just now acquired an imperfection.

SOPHIE: But isn't it perfectly natural to talk about the properties of nonexistent things? Isn't it okay to say that Santa Claus is jolly? Wasn't Huck Finn a runaway?

OSCAR: It would make more sense if when we say "Santa is jolly," what we really mean is that *if* Santa existed, he *would* be jolly. And *if* God existed, then he would be perfect. Existence is presupposed by perfections and imperfections, but it isn't one of them. If we follow your reasoning, then a perfect *anything* can be proved to exist just as easily. I'm sure we could come up with a list of attributes that a perfect unicorn would need to have. Let's see, it has to have four legs; it should look just like a horse; a big horn should be sticking out of its head—and it has to exist! If it didn't, it wouldn't be a perfect unicorn, because I'd be able to conceive of one that did exist.

DAVID: I hate to admit it, Sophie, but I have to agree with Oscar on this one. It really does seem that you could prove the existence of a perfect anything with this argument.

SOPHIE: It's not that simple. Perfection is not part of the definition of a unicorn—

OSCAR: But it's part of the definition of a *perfect* unicorn.

SOPHIE: As I started to say, the central idea is that perfection is essential to this concept of God, but not of unicorns.

OSCAR: I know, I know. But you said yourself, Sophie, that people have had other conceptions of God, and they haven't always been of a perfect being. So let's say that I am now upgrading the traditional conception of a unicorn by conceiving of the most perfect conceivable unicorn. Now that I have conceived of it, by your reasoning it must exist.

SOPHIE: As I see it, when you talk about the most perfect conceivable unicorn, you're talking about what would be a perfect specimen of a unicorn, if unicorns existed at all. But when you talk about God as the most perfect conceivable being, you're not saying what God would be like if beings existed at all. The idea is not that God is the most perfect conceivable member of some general category; it's a conception of God according to which *nothing* of any sort whatever can be conceived to be more perfect. So the parallel to the unicorn example is only superficial.

OSCAR: I still don't trust this argument. It just doesn't seem right to build existence into the definition of a thing, even if you do it indirectly. You're saying that God is, by definition, so perfect that one can't even conceive of a more perfect being. Then you're saying that that definition logically implies that he exists, because if he didn't he'd be less perfect than he could conceivably be. That's the part that I can't go along with. As far as I'm concerned, you can adjust your definitions of God and perfection as much as you want, but it's all still "on paper," if you know what I mean. I don't think that its being defined can prove the existence of anything.

SOPHIE: What about you, David? What do you think?

DAVID: I don't know. As a believer, of course I'm tempted to go along with any argument that tries to show that God exists, but this one seems very tricky. I like the idea of making perfection part of the concept of God, because it implies something more than a creator; it also implies moral perfection. But for showing that God exists, it just isn't the way I tend to think about it.

SOPHIE: I wanted to give you a break from Oscar's badgering. The thing I find intriguing about this argument is that it contains the seed of a very interesting idea: that God would create a universe in which the only clue to his existence would be planted in our own minds. It's as if the very fact that people have developed this idea about God somehow points to his existence.

OSCAR: It may be interesting, but for purposes of convincing a skeptic, I think you should try something else.

DAVID: Back to the drawing board, I guess. I have some other ideas, but I need some time to work them out.

SOPHIE: Wait a minute. I want to try a different approach to the idea of God's leaving conceptual clues to his existence in our minds.

OSCAR: Sure; leave no stone unturned. What's the new angle?

SOPHIE: Can you accept the idea that a contingent being depends on some other being for its existence?

OSCAR: I'm not sure what you mean. What's a "contingent being"?

SOPHIE: It's something that could exist or might not exist. It doesn't *have* to exist.

OSCAR: Okay, I'm with you.

SOPHIE: Well, your own existence depends on the existence of your parents. If they had never existed, you wouldn't either.

OSCAR: I have no problem with that, but it sounds like we're heading back to the first-cause argument.

SOPHIE: Maybe, but I think this argument is more powerful. Let's switch levels for a moment. Let's talk about the fact that you exist. Would you agree that this fact depends on other facts, such as the fact that your parents existed?

OSCAR: I don't know what you mean by "switching levels." It sounds like you're just saying the same thing again, but in any case I agree.

SOPHIE: I call it switching levels because it's a move from talking about things to talking about facts about things. Now think about this: Don't most facts depend on other facts?

OSCAR: I suppose so. You could say that one thing is true just because certain other things are true, assuming that a truth is the same thing as a fact. Is that what you mean?

SOPHIE: Yes. So we'll say that facts that depend on other facts are *contingent*. Now it's fairly clear that if all facts are contingent, then there's an infinite regress. Every fact would depend on an infinite number of other facts.

OSCAR: Let me see if I understand this. The fact that I am male depends on certain other facts, such as my genetic makeup, and so on. That makes it contingent, because if some of those other things had been different, I wouldn't be male. So now you're saying that if *every* fact is contingent, then for anything at all to be true, an infinite number of other things would have to be true. What's wrong with that?

SOPHIE: Maybe nothing is wrong with it. I'm just trying to work through this idea of contingency. Think about this: If in order to *know* some fact you have to know the facts that it depends on, then it would be a problem if all facts are contingent. It would mean that to know anything you have to know infinitely many things.

DAVID: I can see why that would be a problem. Maybe it means that we can't really know anything. On the other hand, maybe we don't have to know everything that a fact depends on in order to know that fact. I know it's a fact that the sun is shining today, but I'm sure that fact depends on a lot of things that I don't have a clue about.

OSCAR: David is right. I don't think we need to know *why* the sun is shining to know that it *is* shining. So where were you going with this?

SOPHIE: I was leading up to the possibility that there are facts that aren't contingent.

OSCAR: What is that supposed to mean?

SOPHIE: It means that maybe some facts are *necessarily* so, not just contingently so.

OSCAR: Can you give an example or two?

SOPHIE: There are different kinds of necessary truths. Some are things that are true by definition, such as "No triangle has four sides." Others are true because of their logical form; for example, "Either that animal is a dog or it isn't." But here's a different kind of example from Greek philosophy: "Anything extended in space could, in principle, be subdivided into two parts that are both extended in space." It doesn't appear to be true by definition or as a result of its logical form; it's *conceptually* necessary that it be true.

OSCAR: Is that a fancy way of saying that anything can be cut in half?

SOPHIE: Not exactly. Cutting is a physical operation, and the Greeks understood that there are definite limits to how far you can take such operations. Still, even if you consider something that you can't possibly cut in half, such as an electron, if it has dimensions to begin with, then you can at least conceive of its being subdivided into parts that have dimensions. Half-electrons may not be physically possible, but the idea is coherent.

OSCAR: Okay, so you want to say that this is an example of a fact that isn't contingent, right?

SOPHIE: It's supposed to be an example of a necessary truth, a truth that doesn't depend on any other truth and couldn't even be conceived not to be true.

OSCAR: You're saying that I can't even conceive of its not being true that anything can be subdivided. I'll accept that for now. Keep going.

SOPHIE: Let's go back to facts about the existence of things. If you look at the various things in the universe, the fact that any one of them exists is a contingent fact. It depends on other facts.

OSCAR: Okay, I think you said that already. Now what?

SOPHIE: If the existence of each thing in the universe is a contingent fact, it's hard to see how the existence of the universe itself could be other than a contingent fact. I mean, how could you get a necessary truth by summing a lot of contingent facts? In theory you could make a list of everything that exists in the universe, and for each one you could state the fact that it exists. Each one of those facts, or truths, would be contingent. If you connected them all together, you'd still just have one long contingent truth.

OSCAR: Not only that, Sophie, but that one long truth would not be anything different from the lots of little contingent facts that make it up. You don't get a new truth by joining together lots of individual facts.

DAVID: But where does that get us? If the existence of the universe itself is a contingent fact, so what?

SOPHIE: So the existence of the universe would have to depend on something that is not contingent. Because if you say that it depends on something contingent, then that fact just gets added to the list of contingent facts about the universe. Here's another way to put it: If the universe itself is a contingent being, then it must depend for its existence on a necessary being, something that *must* exist, by its very nature. The universe itself doesn't have that sort of nature, so something else must have.

OSCAR: Let me guess. God?

DAVID: Bravo! The man wins a coffee.

SOPHIE: There it is, Oscar. The idea is that God is the *only* being that *necessarily* exists.

OSCAR: That's interesting, Sophie. It's the best I've heard so far. There's one thing that bothers me, though.

DAVID: The fact that you can't think of a refutation?

OSCAR: Slow down; I'm not finished yet. I want to know where we get this neat division of facts into contingent and necessary.

Who says that all facts fall into one of these two categories?

SOPHIE: What else could there be? Either a fact depends on another fact or it doesn't. There's no middle position.

OSCAR: Okay, I can see that, but maybe all the "not dependent" facts don't belong together.

SOPHIE: How would you separate them?

OSCAR: I'd make room for facts that aren't dependent on other facts, but aren't necessary truths either. I wouldn't assume that "not dependent" means "necessary."

SOPHIE: I think I follow you so far, but where are you going with this?

OSCAR: First, let me ask you this: How are we supposed to know whether a truth is necessary?

SOPHIE: A necessary truth couldn't conceivably be false. It is, in that sense, self-evident. If you try to conceive of it as false, you end up contradicting yourself, because its truth is built right into the concepts that compose it. That means that to know that it's true, you don't have to know anything but the meaning of those concepts; you don't have to know any other facts about the world. But a contingent truth can be conceived to be false without any self-contradiction, because the reason why it is true involves other facts. What I'm leading up to is something called the Principle of Sufficient Reason.

OSCAR: And what might that be?

SOPHIE: It's the principle that there must be a *reason* for the truth of every fact, either built into the concepts of the fact itself, as in necessary truth, or resting in some other fact.

OSCAR: Here's what bothers me. This principle seems to be saying that the universe must be set up so that it makes sense. Everything has a reason or is self-evident. That strikes me as arrogant, frankly.

DAVID: What's arrogant about it, Oscar?

OSCAR: Well, who *says* that everything is so nicely structured? Why couldn't there be such things as *brute facts,* facts that don't depend on other facts but aren't self-explanatory either; that just *are?* Who can say that the existence of the universe itself isn't just such a brute fact?

SOPHIE: Brute facts would be fundamentally inexplicable then, right?

OSCAR: I suppose so. Why not?

SOPHIE: This would concede that there is no explanation possible for why there is a universe at all. It just *is.*

OSCAR: Maybe that's just the way things are. There's no law that says reality has to make the kind of sense that we recognize. It doesn't have to make sense at all.

DAVID: That's true, Oscar, but as I've been listening to you two, the whole thing has taken the form of a dilemma in my mind. It's like this: Either God exists or the universe is inexplicable. That's what it boils down to, isn't it?

OSCAR: Right. And there's nothing to force me to accept the claim that God exists.

DAVID: Sure, but then another way to put it would be this: If the universe is not inexplicable, then God exists. That's just a simple logical transformation of the original dilemma. So really the ultimate question is whether or not the universe is explicable.

OSCAR: How should I know whether it is or it isn't? All I know is that it *might* not be, so I need not believe in God.

DAVID: I'm just not sure how a rational line of thinking could lead to the conclusion that there's no rational reason why anything exists at all. You started out by saying that belief in God is irrational, but now it looks as if the universe itself is irrational if God doesn't exist.

OSCAR: Not so fast, David. For a rational mind there is no requirement to believe in an ultimately rational universe. It is not irrational to say that the kind of sense that we can make of the world is—how should I put it?—*local* instead of ultimate. Our kind of rationality is the outcome of our evolutionary history, in the course of which it has paid off to try to understand things. That doesn't mean that everything has to turn out to be understandable.

SOPHIE: The argument has taken a pretty interesting turn. It really comes down to a question of one's basic orientation to the world. If Oscar is right and there is no God, then the universe is ultimately indifferent to our sense of order and intelligibility. In fact, it is worse than indifferent; it's *foreign* to reason, and we are therefore foreign to it. After all, the Principle of Sufficient Reason is a pretty deeply intuitive principle. If it is false, then it would not be far wrong to say that our kind of intelligence doesn't *belong* in this universe.

OSCAR: That's very poetic, Sophie, but I think you may be

overstating the case somewhat. I mean, it could be that there is enough sense and order in the universe to give our minds something to hang on to even if it is ultimately inexplicable. Besides, shouldn't we ask about the Principle of Sufficient Reason itself? If it is true, what sort of truth is it: necessary or contingent?

SOPHIE: I think the whole point of the principle is that it should be recognized as a necessary truth about what might be called the "logical structure" of the universe.

OSCAR: So it's a necessary truth? It doesn't seem so to me. After all, David's dilemma concedes that it *might* be false. Either God exists or the universe is inexplicable and the Principle of Sufficient Reason is false. If it were a necessary truth, then it wouldn't make sense to suppose that it might be false. And if it's contingent, what truth does it depend on? It can't be a brute fact, because the whole point of the principle is that there are no brute facts. So the problem is that the Principle of Sufficient Reason entails that every truth is either necessary or contingent, but the principle itself is neither. That means it isn't true at all.

SOPHIE: That's very slick, Oscar; maybe a little bit too slick. David, however, didn't state that the Principle of Sufficient Reason might be false. He said either God exists or the universe is inexplicable. Another way to set it up is like this: If the Principle of Sufficient Reason is true, then God exists. You have pointed out that if it's true at all, it has to be a necessary truth, but that's okay with this argument. The fact that it's part of that dilemma doesn't mean that it's not a necessary truth. That's a separate question, one that's just as deep as the question about God. It seems that the two questions are tightly linked, though. This argument doesn't settle the question about God, but it certainly does show a lot about what the commitments are on either side of it.

DAVID: Yes, and even though the question is still open, this whole discussion somehow clarifies my own faith for me. It's as if at some level I must choose how to relate to the world: as a place either where my mind belongs or where it doesn't belong. I can't know for sure, but I find myself incapable of believing that the universe doesn't make sense. I can entertain the idea, but I can't believe it.

SOPHIE: Not only that, but the Principle of Sufficient Reason has been a part of the scientific worldview for a long time, in the sense that scientists are committed not only to figuring out the way the world is but also the *reasons* why it is that way. This doesn't mean that scientists think they have the universe all figured out, or even that they think they someday will. But it does represent a kind of ideal that they believe in. Oscar, you have been fond of saying that a belief in God is not compatible with a scientific outlook, but science also presupposes that the universe makes sense and that we can understand it. The Greeks gave us the idea of *cosmos*, an ordered, intelligible universe in which things happen for a reason. It appears that the idea of cosmos is at the heart of both science and religion.

OSCAR: I'll need to hear more than this before I am convinced.

Chapter 4

The Natural Order

It is the following day. Oscar, David, and Sophie meet for lunch in the cafeteria. David is eager to resume their conversation of the day before.

OSCAR: So, you have it all figured out, David?

DAVID: I have a better idea of how to proceed. The argument I have in mind seems much more powerful than anything we discussed yesterday, and I think it will appeal to your scientific temperament, Oscar.

OSCAR: Well, don't keep us in suspense. Let's hear it.

DAVID: Let me start with an analogy. First, imagine that you are walking through a forest. This forest is completely wild, untouched by any human presence.

OSCAR: I guess I'll have to imagine it. There's not much chance of actually finding such a place anymore.

DAVID: Right. As I was saying, you're walking through this forest, admiring its sheer wildness. Then you come upon a spot that is very different; and the difference is quite obvious. Here, the bushes are in neat rows, their branches all of the same length. The blades of grass are short and all of the same length, too. There are no loose twigs or leaves lying around. The area is exactly square in shape, and in the center are flowers of different colors. The flowers are arranged in concentric circles, with each band containing flowers of a single color. The bed of flowers is ringed by smooth white rocks. What is the first thing you think, when you find this place?

OSCAR: I would think that you were lying to me about its being untouched by any human presence. Obviously it's a garden.

DAVID: And what does that tell you?

OSCAR: It doesn't tell me anything, except that someone is

31

pretty rich to be able to afford this fancy garden out in the middle of nowhere. Pretty rich or pretty crazy.

DAVID: Wait, I'm serious. What makes you so sure this is a garden?

OSCAR: It's obvious, the way you described it. Somebody, a gardener, had to mow the grass, plant and trim the bushes, rake the leaves, and arrange the flowers. A garden can't tend itself. I'm beginning to see the point of your analogy.

DAVID: Good. I think it should be clear by now what I'm driving at. If there's one thing that science tells us about the universe, it's that it is an orderly place. Every scientific law of nature states a principle of order, drawing a line between the possible and the impossible. What is it that made you so sure you had wandered into a garden? It's the fact that gardens are orderly. And you said yourself that things don't just get into that kind of arrangement by accident; somebody has to put them there and keep them there. A gardener, you said it was. Well, science reveals order, or design, in the universe. It's not a place where things just happen any which way. They happen in an orderly, predictable way. It follows that the universe didn't get this way by itself. There had to be a Designer, a Master Gardener. That's God.

OSCAR: Very good, David. I have to admit, that's a much stronger argument. At the moment I can't see anything really wrong with it, although I'm sure I'll find something. I do have one question, though. Isn't order a pretty subjective thing? You know, when I go to my car mechanic, her place looks disorderly to me; there's junk piled everywhere. To her, it's very orderly; she knows exactly where everything is.

DAVID: Maybe that kind of order is subjective, but physicists work with the concept of order all the time. For example, if you blow a smoke ring, it gradually but inevitably scatters and fades away, even in a still room. That's because of the motion of the air molecules. It takes seconds, or perhaps minutes, to happen. But even if you wait around for a very long time, you won't see that ring form in the air again, even though the molecules of the smoke are still hanging in the air. That's because the ring is a very orderly arrangement; scattered smoke isn't. The second law of thermodynamics says that the amount of disorder in the universe is steadily increasing. It explains the smoke ring; it explains why cars break down, why pictures fade, why we get old, die, and decompose—

OSCAR: Couldn't we repeal this law?

DAVID: There's one person who could do something about it, if you're interested.

OSCAR: I should have known better than to ask.

DAVID: The point was to show that the concept of order has a perfectly legitimate scientific use.

OSCAR: Well, David, I have to admit it: You've really done your homework this time.

SOPHIE: I have a few questions about this argument, David.

DAVID: Sure. Go ahead.

SOPHIE: For one thing, this is an analogy; you were supposed to give a proof.

DAVID: What's wrong with using an analogy?

SOPHIE: There's nothing wrong with it as part of an argument, but you have to be careful about how you use it. Saying that one thing is similar to another in ways that we can observe can help us to observe the thing more clearly, or in a new way. But when you *extend* the analogy beyond what can be observed, your argument rests on the assumption that the two things continue to be similar. In this case, the observable similarity is the orderliness of the garden and the orderliness of the universe. The inference to a gardener is also very safe, because we have observed that gardens are made by gardeners. The inference to a Master Designer of the universe rests on the assumption that the similarity between the two goes beyond what is observable.

OSCAR: Bull's-eye! I wish I'd thought of that. I apologize for all those nasty things I said about your being a secret theist, Sophie.

SOPHIE: All in search of truth, Oscar.

DAVID: I don't see the problem. Scientists use analogies all the time. They speak of gravity as being like a dent in space-time, or organic molecules as being like pieces of a jigsaw puzzle. If they can do it, why can't I? Furthermore, this appears to be a perfect example of the kind of reasoning you say is appropriate for proving the existence of an unobservable being.

SOPHIE: For one thing, these scientific analogies are just illustrations, used to make difficult concepts easier to understand. They also are very useful for helping to generate hypotheses. I'm not saying that analogies are *bad*, only that they must be supported. In this case, you need to tell us more about the concept of order and why it requires an order-maker; only then will we be able to tell if the analogy is a good one.

DAVID: Okay, I'll grant you that the analogy between the garden and the universe isn't by itself conclusive, but I think it captures the logic of the argument very well. As you say, it's an illustration that makes the basic idea easier to understand.

SOPHIE: And the basic idea again is . . . ?

DAVID: Let me put it this way. Physics is the science that looks for the most basic laws of nature. Although physics isn't finished, it has discovered many things. If you look in a physics book, you'll find statements like $F = ma$ or $E = mc^2$—things like that. Even though they are written as mathematical equations, they are really statements about the universe. Each says something different, but they all manage to say one thing very clearly: In this universe, things don't just happen any old which way. There are patterns to events, patterns that we can see and understand. That's how we're able to use these statements to predict things. Well, a pattern is just another word for order. The universe is an orderly place.

SOPHIE: And how is that supposed to prove that God exists?

DAVID: I've already told you. Order is a very improbable state of affairs. The law of entropy shows that. Once we recognize the orderliness of the universe, reason demands that we recognize it as the work of an intelligent Being. Forget about the garden and the gardener; we're talking now about reason.

SOPHIE: You've stated the argument very forcefully, David. What do you think, Oscar? Has David made his case?

OSCAR: As I said before, this is much more impressive than the other two "proofs." Still, there's something about it that bothers me. I have this funny feeling that the word "order" is being used in two different senses, and that one of them isn't quite right.

DAVID: What do you mean? I thought I gave a reasonably scientific explanation of order.

OSCAR: You did. You talked about smoke rings and entropy, and you showed that certain kinds of processes in nature seem to happen in one direction. The smoke ring doesn't form again in midair, because a ring is a more orderly situation than a smoky room, right?

DAVID: Right.

OSCAR: If you wanted to get that smoke back into a ring, you'd have to do some fancy collecting and filtering; it would take a lot of energy and work. Your idea is that it would take a similar amount of work to put the universe into its orderly pattern, following nice, neat physical laws, and all that. And God, as you see it, is the source of all this.

DAVID: I couldn't have said it better myself.

OSCAR: I know. Well, here's my first salvo. When you talk about order and smoke rings, you are presupposing that the laws of nature are what they are.

DAVID: What do you mean?

OSCAR: The fact that a smoke ring is more orderly than a smoky room in this universe is a consequence of the kind of natural laws that are in effect in it. Maybe there could be a different universe, with different laws, where the smoke ring wouldn't be more orderly.

DAVID: Maybe that's possible, but we're talking about *this* universe, with the laws we know about.

OSCAR: Here's the problem. "Order," as you've explained it, only makes sense given a set of physical laws. Those laws are the rules that we observe *in* nature. The order that we observe is actually described by those laws.

DAVID: Why is it a problem?

SOPHIE: Just a minute; this isn't right. That a smoke ring is orderly is *not* because of natural laws; it's a result of the fact that it satisfies the concept of order. The natural laws are just the explanation of how it is possible for it to do that.

OSCAR: What do you mean by "satisfying the concept of order"? This sounds like an evasion.

SOPHIE: Not at all. The smoke ring has a kind of structure to it that the smoky room doesn't have. That structure is what makes it orderly.

OSCAR: Says who? Why not say that the smoky room is just a different kind of structure, a different kind of order?

SOPHIE: Let's make it simpler. Imagine a large checkerboard, and then just drop some checkers onto the squares, randomly.

Oscar: Okay, no problem.

Sophie: Now, if I asked you to tell me the "state" of that checkerboard, how would you go about it?

Oscar: You mean the actual configuration of checkers? I'd just tell you where they are.

Sophie: Yes, but how would you do that?

Oscar: Let's see, I guess I'd assign letters and numbers to the squares and say "There's a checker at C-5, and another one at E-20," and so on until I got them all.

Sophie: Right. That would work. This time, imagine the same checkerboard, but with the checkers arranged in a circle. How would you describe the state of the checkerboard this time?

Oscar: If I wanted to, I could do the same thing again: Give you the coordinates of each checker.

Sophie: That's right, you could do that; but you wouldn't have to. You could describe the configuration much more compactly by saying something like, "The checkers are arranged in a circle with a diameter of 20 squares around square D-15."

Oscar: Yes, I could do that too.

Sophie: That's what makes it a more orderly state—the fact that it can be described by a method more precise than just pointing out the position of each component. That's a *conceptual* property of the state, and it applies to the smoke ring as well as the ring of checkers. We don't need to consider the actual physical laws until we try to figure out how smoke rings happen in the first place, and why they don't last very long. I would argue that the *concept* of order would apply in any universe that we can conceive of, even though the particular order that we might find could be different.

Oscar: Okay, I stand corrected. I still think there's a problem with this argument. We all agree that there's an order in nature. And now, Sophie, you have shown that order itself is a conceptual property. But a few minutes ago David said that order is *improbable* and that the law of entropy tells us so. But let's look at this again. What we know is that in this universe, with the kind of order that it has, orderly states are improbable because disorder, or entropy, is always increasing. I don't argue with that. I start to have problems when you say that *order itself* is improbable. I don't know where you're getting that from, but I'm pretty sure there's nothing in thermodynamics or entropy to support it.

DAVID: Let me try it again. We agree that the laws of nature could be different from what they are, but the universe would still be orderly, only it would have a different kind of order. My argument is that the fact that the universe is orderly at all implies a kind of order *behind* the universe, something that *originates* the order. Maybe "improbable" is the wrong word, but what I'm getting at is that the presence of *any kind of order at all* in the universe implies an order-giver.

OSCAR: I get it. But I am arguing that you have transferred this inference from order to an order-giver to a domain where it has no meaning. Sure, when we find order within nature, we look for an order-giver, because the kind of order that we have here makes that a good bet. We look *in* nature for the source of the instances of order that we find. When we shift from the order within nature to the existence of order itself and start speculating about the order behind nature, all bets are off.

SOPHIE: Why don't we just say that David shouldn't use an argument based on improbability to get at his order, or order-giver, behind nature? Maybe we should look for another line of reasoning that is more promising. I'd like to get back to the main point: whether reason demands that this orderly universe had a Designer.

OSCAR: Fine. You take over, Sophie. Between the two of us, we ought to be able to wear him down.

SOPHIE: Truth, Oscar; let's not forget about the truth. That's what we're looking for, not David's surrender.

DAVID: I'm not sure I can always tell the difference.

SOPHIE: Well, let me try another approach. Suppose you said to me, "Sophie, you got your hair cut." What would that pre-suppose?

DAVID: What do you mean? It would presuppose that you got your hair cut, that's all.

SOPHIE: No, you don't understand. How would you be in a position to know that I got my hair cut?

DAVID: Well, I'd notice that it was shorter than it had been.

SOPHIE: Exactly. It presupposes that you know how I would look if I hadn't gotten my hair cut. Here's the payoff. When you talk about the universe being orderly, that presupposes that you have some conception of what a disorderly universe would be like. I think part of Oscar's claim is that you have no such idea, so your claim about the order of the universe isn't really meaning-ful, after all.

DAVID: That's not such a deadly criticism, Sophie; I was expect-ing a real torpedo. As a matter of fact, I can think of a good response.

SOPHIE: Great. Let's hear it.

DAVID: Fine. Let me make sure I understand what you're get-ting at. You believe that in order for the claim that the universe is orderly to be meaningful, it presupposes that I can conceive of a universe without order. Since I can't do that, according to you I don't really know what I'm saying when I say the universe is orderly.

SOPHIE: That's about the size of it.

DAVID: But I do have a perfectly good idea of what a disorderly universe would be like. It would be chaos. I can conceive of chaos. In a perfectly chaotic universe, there would be no pattern to events; things would just happen. There would be no life, since life is very orderly. There wouldn't even be matter. There would be no basic particles, no constant entities of any sort. Stuff would just wink in and out of existence, with nothing resembling any-thing else. That's what I mean by "chaos."

SOPHIE: I'm just wondering whether this would really be chaos, or just a different kind of order—maybe a kind we can't under-stand.

DAVID: I think you're making it harder than it has to be, Sophie. I don't think I'm going too far out on a limb to say that for order to exist, there must be entities that exist over time that behave according to laws that exist over time. I grant you that there might be many different ways to meet those conditions, but I don't think it's that difficult to conceive of a universe that fails to meet them.

In fact, I could even use the argument that you just used with Oscar. In an orderly universe, things can be described by their structures and mathematical patterns; in a chaotic universe, they can't. I can say that this universe is orderly because it satisfies the concept of order, and it does so by behaving in ways that can be compactly described by mathematical statements. So I don't buy the argument that says I can't talk about this universe being orderly because I don't have any other universes to compare it with.

SOPHIE: Okay, I withdraw the argument. Let me switch for a minute to the order that we do find within nature. We all seem to be in agreement that as time goes on, the amount of entropy in the universe is increasing. We are going from a more ordered universe to a less ordered one.

DAVID: Yes, that's right.

SOPHIE: I'm wondering whether you also intend this as another argument for the existence of God. If, as we head into the future, we can expect to find less and less order, then as we look into the past we should expect to find more and more order, until we come to God.

DAVID: That's a different argument from the one I've been thinking about, although I've heard something like it before. I never cared for the image of God "winding up" the universe like a watch, then letting it unwind into entropy, but I suppose there's nothing logically wrong with it.

SOPHIE: I just wanted to be clear that that wasn't the argument you had in mind. And in fact I think there are some serious objections to it. Think of a completely shuffled deck of cards. Even if I grant that a thoroughly shuffled deck is disorderly, if I keep shuffling I can get some relatively ordered configurations, can't I?

OSCAR: That's what makes poker interesting, Sophie.

DAVID: Thank you, Oscar. Sure, Sophie, even chaos can have temporary stretches of order, as long as they're temporary.

SOPHIE: Maybe the universe is like that. Maybe it was around for an infinitely long time in a completely chaotic state. Then, about fifteen billion years ago, a random but orderly event occurred: what we call the "beginning" of the universe. Now, from this perspective, the orderly history of the universe as we know it is just a minor fluctuation in the stream of chaos. It's strictly temporary, since, as you pointed out, the second law of thermodynamics tells us that order in the universe is on its way out. We happen to live in this fluctuation, so we think of it as the whole picture. We could be wrong; the universe could be one tiny little island of order in a sea of eternal chaos. Looked at in this way, the universe doesn't require any divine intervention—just random processes and plenty of time.

OSCAR: That's pretty heavy, Sophie. I like it.

DAVID: I can't imagine that you actually believe it.

SOPHIE: It's not a question of believing it or not believing it, David. If it's merely *possible* that a temporary interval of order could exist in a generally chaotic universe, then it isn't *necessary* for there to be a God to do the "initial" ordering, because there didn't have to be any initial ordering. So the observed increase in entropy doesn't point back to a God who "wound up" the world.

DAVID: But that's such a farfetched counterexample.

SOPHIE: That has nothing to do with logic. Besides, who are we to say what's farfetched and what isn't? Our understanding of the universe is based on the fifteen billion years that we think we know something about. If time is infinite—and we have no reason to suppose that it isn't—then fifteen billion years is a drop in the bucket. To put it another way, if you have infinite time to wait, eventually the smoke in that room will form a nice ring in the air, without any help from anybody.

DAVID: I see the point now. That's a fairly depressing vision of reality, but it's only a side issue. My argument is about the fact of order in the universe at all, even the winding-down kind of order. If that kind of order implies that God exists, then we might have grounds for questioning whether God would be in the business of creating a cosmic wind-up toy.

OSCAR: I still don't find anything very decisive in all this. We've established that the universe is a place that has order in it. The comparison of that to a garden with a gardener is an interesting allegory, but not a rigorous argument. But cheer up, David. It's not your fault that there are no good proofs for the existence of God.

DAVID: Thanks a lot. The trouble is, I feel as if it is my fault. I should be able to do a better job with this.

SOPHIE: Don't despair. I know that I've learned a great deal from these discussions. In fact, I have to admit that there is a sort of variant on the Argument from Design that has always appealed to me.

DAVID: Really? What variant is that? It seems to me that you and Oscar have really hammered the argument.

SOPHIE: I don't think this would count as a proof, but it has to do with evolution itself. I have always been struck by the fact that humans seem to be overendowed with certain capacities.

OSCAR: What do you mean, "overendowed"?

SOPHIE: Our minds have evolved to the level where we can do physics, higher mathematics, philosophy. There's the music of Mozart, the poetry of Shakespeare, the game of chess, and so on. The gap between the repertoire of the human mind and those of the minds of the rest of the species on this planet is just so wide that it's hard to believe that natural selection has driven us to this level. Our minds just seem to be far more evolved than they need to be.

OSCAR: How do we really know that? Maybe we needed to reach a certain level of intelligence to survive, and all these other abilities are just side effects of reaching that level. We don't have to suppose that evolution selected the ability to write string quartets, after all—an ability that most of us don't have anyway.

SOPHIE: Of course. My "argument" is more an intuition, anyway. It's as if evolution could account for a certain number of our abilities, but as for the rest, there seems to be something actually uplifting us, upstepping our abilities in some way. The image I have is evolution pushing us upward from below, while something else pulls us from above.

OSCAR: That's a poetic image, but I don't think there's much scientific support for it. We're just not in a position to say that plain old natural selection *can't* account for this or that aspect of human behavior.

DAVID: Then we should be cautious about saying that it *must* account for all aspects. I never really thought of Sophie's point about evolution before, but it at least opens up the argument a little, which I think is a good thing.

SOPHIE: And think about this. Scientists are pretty sure that the ability to fly evolved several times, independently, in different parts of the world and under different conditions. Another example of this is the evolution of eyes and vision, which have evolved in different species independently. And there are many more examples of parallel evolution.

OSCAR: Is this supposed to imply that these things were the result of intelligent planning? To me, it only implies that what works for one species can work for another species, and that

natural selection will usually evoke the best solution to a problem. I'm sure there must be some species that didn't make it
because they *couldn't* evolve into flying or seeing creatures, or
whatever.

SOPHIE: That's not where I was going with my line of thinking,
Oscar. I agree with you that natural selection can account for
parallel evolution. In fact, the theory of evolution by natural
selection would lead you to *expect* parallel evolution, for just the
reasons you gave. What has always seemed strange to me, however, is that reason—the full-fledged abstract, symbol-using
activity that we call reason—has evolved only once. But reason
has been so successful for us that you would expect natural
selection to have endowed at least a few other species with it.
Why just humans?

OSCAR: Hey, evolution isn't over yet. Maybe other species *will*
achieve reason. We humans haven't had it that long, in evolutionary terms. It seems like a big jump to me to conclude that
human rationality is a divine gift rather than an evolutionary
achievement.

SOPHIE: I wasn't thinking of it as a gift so much as a kind of
planned upstepping, a boost. And I can take this sort of argument
a step further. Try this: The more we learn about the mind, the
more we are finding out that most of the important stuff happens
unconsciously.

OSCAR: What do you mean by the "important stuff"?

SOPHIE: I mean the information processing, problem solving,
judging, evaluating. As an example, think about what happens
when you meet and recognize someone whom you haven't seen
in years.

OSCAR: Well, what's interesting about it? You recognize the
person, and that's that.

SOPHIE: Right, but my point is that you don't know a thing
about *how* that happens. You are conscious only that you do
recognize the person. But when you think about it, you realize
that in order for this to happen, a very sophisticated identification
process had to take place. That process, however, is not a conscious one. Increasingly, cognitive scientists are discovering that
this is the rule, not the exception.

OSCAR: What does this have to do with God?

SOPHIE: I'm leading up to that. The first thing this points to is that consciousness isn't all that important.

DAVID: How can you say that? It seems to me that if I lose consciousness—permanently—I lose something *very* important.

SOPHIE: Of course consciousness is important to *us*, because it's fundamental to what we are. But when you look at it from a more detached scientific viewpoint, it's not clear what consciousness is *for*.

DAVID: I still don't think I get it.

SOPHIE: Okay, try this. Our behavior is what gets us into trouble or gets us out of trouble. Behavior is controlled by mental processes that are coming to be understood as information processes—computations. These processes don't require consciousness. Therefore, consciousness is an "extra," a kind of frill. We could just as well have evolved without it.

DAVID: If we had evolved without consciousness, we'd just be zombies. Is that what you are saying?

SOPHIE: That's it. For evolutionary purposes, we could have turned out to be zombies. We would be *rational* zombies, insentient beings that behave in intelligent ways. But we're not zombies; therefore consciousness is an "overendowment."

OSCAR: Congratulations, Sophie, for producing what is turning out to be the strangest argument I've ever heard. Were you going to connect this to the existence of God at some point?

SOPHIE: Here's the connection. This argument says that there is no obvious reason why consciousness should exist in the universe, so the fact that it does exist calls for a special kind of explanation. The existence of consciousness means that certain parts of the universe—namely us—can *experience* other parts of it. This is a mystery that doesn't have a natural explanation, so it opens the possibility of a supernatural one. A universe with consciousness in it seems greater somehow than one without it. A universe without God doesn't need to maximize "greatness," for lack of a better word, but this is what you would expect in a God-created universe.

OSCAR: You've been studying too hard, Sophie. Take a few days off. Go to the movies.

DAVID: Sophie, I *like* that argument. I need to think about it a lot more, but the whole idea of overendowment is a different kind of "order" that I hadn't considered. It's similar to something I've thought about human morality at its best. We have these ideals, such as loving one's neighbor as oneself, that are very powerful, even though we don't often live up to them. It's hard to imagine these lofty moral ideals being just the product of some sort of evolutionary process.

OSCAR: Why not? Other species, such as wolves, have rules for maintaining social order. Why should we be any different?

DAVID: But that's just the point. A principle like loving one's neighbor as oneself just doesn't seem to be reducible to a rule for maintaining social order. It's not really a "rule" at all, even though it sounds like one. It's more like an instruction to seek a higher perspective on one's place in humanity, to rise above the need for rules. That's what I meant by a moral *ideal*.

OSCAR: You can call it a moral ideal if you want. What is that supposed to show?

DAVID: It makes me think about what Sophie said about evolution, in her "overendowment" argument. It's as if evolution is pushing humanity from below to implement rules and social order, but something else is pulling from above to help us formulate and reach for ideals. She used the word "upstepping" to describe the effect, and that's a good way to think of it. Social rules are upstepped to become moral ideals.

OSCAR: Look, David, I can see how this kind of thinking might appeal to you if you already believe that God is real and that he somehow influences human evolution and history. I hope you don't think that it's persuasive to a skeptic, though.

DAVID: No, you're right, Oscar. These sorts of considerations don't amount to a rigorous proof. It's just that Sophie's idea about overendowment got me thinking again about how—well—*unexpected* our moral ideals can seem. But I think we've already seen that when an argument turns on the inexplicability of something, the atheist will always say that it's just inexplicable, period. Oscar will say that the fact that there's no natural explanation for consciousness, or anything else, doesn't give us reason to bring in a supernatural one.

OSCAR: I'm glad to see that you've learned something, David.

SOPHIE: It may just be that the search for a proof was misguided from the start.

OSCAR: That's what I've been saying.

SOPHIE: No it isn't, Oscar. You started out with the claim that belief in God is *irrational;* then we got into the proof thing. Well, it's good that we did, but let's not forget that provability is only one part of what could make a belief rational. There's more to rationality than proof, so the case isn't closed yet.

DAVID: What did you have in mind, Sophie?

SOPHIE: We can talk about it another time. Sooner or later, I'm going to have to go to my classes.

Chapter 5

Suffering

After class, they meet back in the cafeteria. David buys coffee; Oscar is itching to resume the discussion.

OSCAR: You know, Sophie, I've been thinking about the whole "strong" and "weak" atheism thing. I feel a certain personal responsibility to defend the strong atheist position, especially after listening to all these arguments.

DAVID: Remind me again what strong atheism is, Oscar. I want to make sure we are talking about the same thing.

SOPHIE: That's the claim that God *couldn't* exist. What about it, Oscar: Do you think God's nonexistence can be proved?

OSCAR: Yes. In fact I think a pretty strong case can be made that God couldn't exist, at least not the sort of God we have been talking about.

DAVID: What do you mean by that, Oscar? What "sort of God" are you talking about?

OSCAR: I mean a God worth worshiping; a benevolent, omnipotent God. We're supposedly talking about more than a first cause here, or even a Cosmic Architect.

DAVID: That's right. It's God's loving nature that attracts worship, not just his awesomeness. But I don't see how this makes it easier to prove that he doesn't exist.

SOPHIE: I think I see where Oscar is going with this. In fact, I'm surprised that it has taken him this long to get around to it.

OSCAR: Unlike some other things we've been hearing lately, there's nothing especially subtle or difficult or strange about this argument; it's simple and straightforward. I'd bet that everyone has considered it at one time or another, even true believers. It's just that the true believers are better at denial.

DAVID: Denial of what?

OSCAR: Denial of human suffering. I think that's what it comes down to. Pick up the newspaper on any day. Read about the people who are killed or mutilated by other people, struck down by disease, killed or ruined by natural disasters. It's an endless parade of misery, to say nothing of the fact that the end of the parade is death by so-called natural causes, if one is lucky enough to have escaped those other horrors. "Natural causes," of course, is a polite way of referring to the slow deterioration and collapse of the biological system; the irreversible degradation and loss of one's faculties.

DAVID: I can't speak for others, but I certainly don't deny these things.

OSCAR: Maybe you don't, but it's a mystery to me how anyone can believe in an all-powerful, *loving* God, who nevertheless tolerates all this in the universe that he supposedly created and rules. It's more than a mystery; it's damned nonsense. I mean, think about children born with AIDS, who live short, sick lives and die miserable deaths. You want me to believe that a loving, benevolent God looks upon all this, with all the power of the universe at his command to stop it, and does nothing?

DAVID: I admit that it may be hard to understand these things, but I don't see how it proves that God doesn't exist.

OSCAR: Like this. If God really is omnipotent, then he can, if he chooses, prevent or stop all suffering. If he really is benevolent and loving, then he will definitely want to do so. But since we see suffering all around us, it's obvious that he is *not* stopping it. Why not? There are two choices: Either he's not as powerful or he's not as loving as he is cracked up to be. Whichever way you choose, he is not a God worth believing in, as far as I'm concerned. If the omnipotent and loving God that people pray to existed, we wouldn't find suffering in the universe. But we do, so he doesn't. End of argument.

DAVID: It sounds to me like you're blaming all the suffering in the world on God. Don't forget, *we* inflict a lot of suffering on ourselves and one another. God gave us free will, but he is not to blame for what we do with it.

OSCAR: If he's all-powerful, he could have given us free will *and* made it impossible for us to do evil things to each other. He could have created us as free but perfectly benevolent beings.

SOPHIE: Wait a minute. I don't see how it's possible for a being to be free but incapable of choosing evil. That reminds me of the joke about Volkswagen Beetles, when they were first manufactured: "You can have any color you want, as long as it's black."

OSCAR: Are you saying this is too tricky for even an omnipotent God?

SOPHIE: I'm saying that it is self-contradictory to suppose that it could be *impossible* for a being with free will to choose evil. To say that a being has free will is the same as saying that she can choose good or evil. Without both possibilities, there is no freedom. It shouldn't count against God's omnipotence that he can't create self-contradictory things.

OSCAR: Why not? Are you placing limitations on omnipotence?

SOPHIE: No, I'm trying to show that it's not as if a self-contradictory being is a real possibility that God can't actualize. Instead, it's a meaningless jumble of concepts. An omnipotent being can't create four-sided triangles, either, but it has nothing to do with omnipotence. Something with four sides just isn't a triangle, and a being who can't choose evil just isn't free. An omnipotent being can bring about any logically possible state of affairs.

OSCAR: All right. Let's grant, for the sake of getting on with the argument, that if we are going to have free will, then it has to be possible for us to choose evil. It still sounds to me like a high price to pay. I think I'd rather do without free will, but live in a world without suffering. He could have arranged that, couldn't he?

DAVID: He could have, I guess, but I'm glad he didn't. Actually, I'm not sure that I even know what it would mean to "do without" free will. If I didn't have free will, I don't think I would be me, if you see what I mean. In fact, I don't think a being without free will would be *anybody*. Free will is built into what I understand a person to be. Besides, I don't think you are appreciating the full importance of the problems we face in life. As difficult as they can be sometimes, without the problems and challenges there wouldn't be many opportunities for growth, especially moral growth.

OSCAR: What do you mean by "moral growth"?

DAVID: I'm talking about the learning of virtues like courage, compassion, perseverance, and love. If life were never frightening, there would be no reason or opportunity for courage or perseverance. If people were always kind to each other, it would be easy to love them. If there were no pain, there would never be a reason to feel compassion.

OSCAR: Whoa! Apply the brakes! Am I hearing this right? Are you saying that we need suffering so that there will be a chance to learn courage and compassion and the rest of it? Is that really what you are arguing?

DAVID: Yes, pretty much. Is that so bizarre?

OSCAR: Bizarre? It's like saying that we should appreciate tooth decay because it allows dentists to have a job, or that we need serial killers so that detectives will have a chance to develop their skills. That way of looking at things stands reason on its head. Courage is valuable *only because* life can be so difficult. What's more, you made it sound as though love is valuable only if it's difficult. What's the point of that?

DAVID: I think a fair case could be made that a universe with virtues like courage is a better place than a universe without them, as long as the suffering involved in acquiring them is balanced out in the end, somehow. And I'm not trying to say that there's no virtue in loving people who are nice to you. I am saying that it's a high achievement to love someone who is not so nice, and that the universe is a better place for that achievement, however rare it is.

OSCAR: So I guess there must be suffering in heaven, too, right? After all, if there isn't any suffering there, it won't be as great a reality as what we have here, according to your argument. Maybe there will even be worse suffering in heaven, eh?

SOPHIE: I don't know if there is much point in moving the argument in that direction, Oscar. The whole point about afterlife is that it comes *after* this life, and that can change the value of things. You can't just say that if suffering has a point in this life, it must have the same point in the afterlife, unless you know that the afterlife is just like this one in every relevant respect. But you don't know that. It's also possible that the afterlife, if any, presents new challenges to those people who manage to surmount the challenges presented here. Maybe there are other virtues to acquire whose meaning we can't yet grasp.

OSCAR: Fine. But it still seems to me that we are rather over-abundantly supplied with opportunities for moral growth, here and now in this life. There seems to be some suffering, further-more, that offers no opportunity for moral growth because it is invisible. Imagine an orphan child, living in a cardboard box in Mexico City or someplace. She is killed in the night by rats, but the occurrence is so common, and the people around are so pre-occupied with their own misery, that no one experiences moral growth or grows in compassion. It's just another meaningless nightmare. Whose moral growth was paid for by this child's suffering?

DAVID: I don't think it makes sense to try to balance the books in that way, to try to show that each particular instance of suffer-ing "pays for" a particular bit of moral growth. It's like asking which raindrop nurtured which tree. The point is that there are no trees without rain, even if some trees don't grow so tall.

OSCAR: But try explaining that to a dead acorn sprout. And while you're at it, explain how the suffering that brings about all this moral growth is "balanced out in the end," to use your expression. What is that supposed to mean?

DAVID: It means that the suffering that we experience in this life is insignificant in comparison to the rewards of the next life. Part of what makes human suffering seem so unredeemable is that we have trouble seeing beyond it. If this life is indeed all there is, then it's hard to avoid concluding that luck plays at least as large a role as virtue in determining how one's life goes. I'm not going to pretend that awful things don't happen to wonderful people sometimes. If what we can directly see of life is all there is, it's pretty hard to believe in a benevolent God. But if life continues after what we call death, things may look very different.

OSCAR: So there we are. Now not only do we have God's existence to establish, we also have to show that there is life after death. It seems to me that the theist has to juggle quite a few balls at one time.

SOPHIE: Oscar has a point, David. He set out to show that a benevolent and omnipotent God couldn't exist in a world that has as much suffering as this one has. Your reply is that the suffering is a necessary precondition for the existence of a greater good, namely moral growth. That's fine, but you apparently agree that moral growth, in itself, is not sufficient to justify the extent of the suffering that we find in the world, so it must be "balanced out" in a next world. This means that God's existence is not logically independent of the hypothesis that there is an afterlife.

DAVID: I don't think I've ever looked at it that way, but I think that's correct. God and an afterlife of some sort are part of the same worldview. I can't say that I have a clear picture of afterlife; it's one of the things that I think I'll find out about on a "need to know" basis.

OSCAR: If you ask me, it makes the whole God case even less believable than it was before.

SOPHIE: That may be so, Oscar, but if the sort of afterlife that David is talking about is possible at all, then your claim to be able to prove that God does not exist fails. If there could be an afterlife, then suffering could be balanced out in some way, so it's not necessarily the case that an omnipotent, loving God doesn't exist.

OSCAR: But doesn't all this lead to a kind of callousness about human suffering? After all, if the afterlife is so wonderful, why should we work so hard at preserving mortal life? Why should we care about trying to alleviate suffering at all? Why not just ignore it and let God compensate for it later? Didn't you say that suffering is *insignificant?*

DAVID: I can only give my opinion here, but I think that you are terribly mistaken in what you are saying. I said that suffering is insignificant *compared* to the afterlife prospects. Significance is relative. I really don't think that we are meant to look at life as if we already were in the afterlife; we're just supposed to remember that there is such a perspective and that someday we'll have it. It's like when you study hard for an exam, but study the wrong material by mistake and fail the exam. Somebody, like Sophie here, might say, "Don't take it too hard. Someday you'll look back on it and laugh." That's true, but Sophie wouldn't mean that you should find it funny *now.*

SOPHIE: I'm trying to piece together your argument, David, with some other thoughts about suffering. It seems that for your position to make sense, it has to be true that a certain amount of suffering is necessary for some greater good, namely moral growth, and that the net amount of suffering in the world is no greater than it needs to be to bring about that greater good. If there is more suffering than is strictly necessary for moral growth, then that suffering would be pointless. It seems to me that no matter how insignificant suffering might seem from the stand-point of the afterlife, pointless suffering ought not to be tolerated by a benevolent God.

DAVID: It's more complicated than that, Sophie, because our free will means that the net amount of suffering that occurs in the world is in part up to us. We can choose to increase it or decrease it. We believe that it's "God's will" that we try to decrease it. Part of our responsibility as creatures with free will is to assist God in minimizing suffering.

OSCAR: To assist God? He needs our help with this? What if we don't minimize suffering, or if we don't do as much to minimize it as we could?

SOPHIE: It's a paradox, isn't it? If free will is itself one of the greater goods, as David has argued, then the maximum amount of suffering necessary in the world is whatever we choose to settle for.

DAVID: That's why it's sometimes said that we are "co-creators" with God. With each choice that we make, we help to bring the moral universe into being.

OSCAR: This is all very moving, but it really works only for *personal* evil, the suffering that we inflict on each other. When it comes to suffering from natural causes, we are not co-creators. We may be able to help each other out somewhat in the face of this suffering, but there's a lot that we can't do a thing about. As things stand, for example, if you are stricken with Alzheimer's disease, you are on a one-way street to mental disintegration and, after far too much time, death. This is not something we have co-created; it's not the result of anybody's free-will choice, except maybe God's. And this is only one example. Does anybody really want to say that all of the horrific suffering caused by nature is the minimum possible, to give us opportunities for moral growth?

DAVID: But we are given something to strive for, to overcome these natural evils.

OSCAR: No, not this time, David. I won't buy it. If you're going to argue that all of the people who have suffered and died from bacterial diseases are redeemed by the fact that it gave us motivation to develop antibiotics, I'm out of the discussion. It's just too monstrous. Let's grant, for the sake of the argument, that *some* good is achieved by humans striving to protect other humans from natural suffering. I still find it hard to believe that the amount of natural suffering in the world is at the minimum possible level to allow us ample opportunities for moral growth. To be specific, it's very hard for me to accept that if Alzheimer's or rabies had not existed, humanity would have been *deprived* in some way. And I can't picture this benevolent God saying, "Things have been quiet. A good earthquake ought to liven them up. I see one coming, and I think I'll let it rip."

DAVID: But this is just the sort of case where it is important to remember that there is an afterlife—

OSCAR: No. There's a limit to how much suffering you can charge on this afterlife credit card. Unless you want to argue that the afterlife is so wonderful that *any* degree of suffering is insignificant, there must be a maximum justifiable level of that suffering. You seem to want to say that whatever amount of suffering we can't avoid is okay; things will work out in the next world. I find that simply too pat and, frankly, unbelievable.

DAVID: I have to wonder whether we are really in a position to know whether there's more natural suffering in the world than there needs to be. We have fairly limited vision in such matters, after all.

SOPHIE: But David, you don't want to end up in the position that Oscar ridiculed earlier—of becoming callous to suffering because it is necessary.

DAVID: Oh, I agree with that. I just want to point out that we shouldn't assume that we are able to understand the full implications of suffering in the whole scheme of things. It's probably a mistake to expect God's will to be intelligible to us in every detail.

OSCAR: That's certainly convenient. If we run up against a problem, such as the sheer amount of suffering in the world, we can just brush it off as one of those things that we are too puny to understand.

DAVID: That's not what I mean at all. I don't mean that anybody should brush anything off. You are absolutely right, Oscar, to take suffering seriously and to object to any attempt to minimize it. I'm only trying to show that the problems we may have with understanding the full meaning of suffering do not add up to a disproof of God's existence. That would be like saying, "If God had any good reason for allowing suffering, I would know exactly what it is." But God may have reason for encouraging us to cultivate a degree of faith and trust, to let us learn to be content that we have some idea how the existence of suffering can be justified. This doesn't require us to understand everything about it. Maybe God wants to make sure that we *don't* make the mistake of becoming apathetic about suffering.

OSCAR: So he keeps us in the dark?

DAVID: So he lets us find our own way, knowing that eventually we'll understand. It's not so different from the way parents treat children, is it?

SOPHIE: My parents didn't tell me that I was adopted until I was in first grade. Before that, they didn't think I would understand, and they were afraid it would just cause a lot of pain and confusion. It's never easy for one to learn a thing like that, I guess, but in retrospect I think they made the right decision.

DAVID: That's the sort of thing I mean. We have to learn to trust that what is baffling now will make sense in the long run, and to remember that the long run is longer than a mortal lifetime.

SOPHIE: Getting back to the main argument, there's another aspect to the free-will defense that you haven't considered.

DAVID: What is that?

SOPHIE: Human beings may not be the only creatures whose free-will decisions have consequences that cause suffering.

DAVID: What do you mean?

SOPHIE: So far, the discussion has proceeded on the assumption that only God and humans are involved, and all else is the "blind forces" of nature.

OSCAR: Whom else did you have in mind? Ancient alien astronauts?

SOPHIE: Maybe. Actually, I didn't have anybody specific in mind. I just wanted to toss in a reminder that there could be other orders of free-willed beings which are capable of mischief, either intentionally or unintentionally, but are beyond our ability to perceive directly.

OSCAR: You must be pretty desperate to invoke invisible agents to place the blame on for natural disasters. Is that what this argument comes to?

DAVID: I don't think it's necessarily desperate, Oscar, but it does take us pretty far from what an impartial rational person could be expected to accept.

SOPHIE: My point is only that it is a possibility—one that has been recognized in many religions—that we are victims of personal evil in ways that most of us don't recognize.

OSCAR: I'll grant it as a bare possibility, but not as a hypothesis that makes any serious difference to this discussion. To put it another way, if the only way the problem of suffering can be dealt with is to blame some of it on us and the rest on demons, then I'll rest my case.

Sophie: That leaves us then with the question of whether the amount of suffering in the world could or could not be balanced by moral growth and the expectation of an afterlife. It's hard to answer that question in any determinate way. If you are already disposed to take seriously the possibility of an afterlife, then faith will probably help you to accept the suffering that you can't do anything about. If you are not so inclined, it's not likely that you will find a way to reconcile the reality of suffering with the existence of a loving God. So even though the afterlife question is logically separate from the God question, the two seem closely connected in terms of the pull they exert on our beliefs.

Oscar: This is probably why people become believers during childhood, before they've had much chance to become acquainted with suffering.

David: That may be so, Oscar, but it makes the conversion of adults to belief in God even more significant.

Sophie: Maybe we're taking too Western a view of suffering. Couldn't we also suppose that what we call suffering is really an illusion? If that were so, the only *problem* about suffering would be that we believe in it.

David: I don't follow you, Sophie. It's real enough to us, and that's what matters, isn't it?

Sophie: In the Vedanta philosophy of India, the entire visible world, along with everything in it, including pain and pleasure, is called *maya*, or illusion. It's like a dream that we are caught in, one that sometimes becomes nightmarish. If we could wake up, we would discover that we have been with God the whole time, and that the suffering was all part of the dream.

Oscar: It seems to me that if you really believed that, you wouldn't be willing to do much about suffering. Instead, you'd spend all your time trying to wake up. I can see how this could lead to the worst kind of indifference.

David: I have to agree with Oscar, for a change. I have a lot of respect for the Eastern religions, but I don't think I could buy into a philosophy that denies the reality of the world altogether.

Sophie: Still, I think it's important to consider other ways of looking at this. It seems that Buddha also recognized the danger of passivity and fatalism in the Vedanta philosophy, so he re-affirmed the reality of suffering, but explained its cause as grasping at the illusion itself, and the various things in it. So on the Buddhist view, even though suffering is rooted in illusion, it is respected, and the importance of compassion is emphasized.

OSCAR: But unless I misremember my survey of religions course, Buddhism doesn't talk about a God, so it's hard to see how it can help theism with the problem of suffering.

SOPHIE: Well, Buddhism views a personalized God as a symbol that is likely to trap us, so it prefers more impersonal concepts, such as "dharma." But dharma is still a kind of intelligent order in the world, a lot like what theists call "God's will."

OSCAR: It seems to me that you still end up with questions about why God would permit us to be stuck with such a pain-ridden dream or illusion. I suppose you could say that something like an "intelligent order" doesn't have to be benevolent in the sense that we have been discussing, but then that would mean that to solve the problem of suffering we still have to pull back from theism as it is usually understood, which was my point in the first place. I'll save the arguments against nontheistic religion for another time.

SOPHIE: I guess you're right. It doesn't really help the case for theism to offer a Buddhist alternative. I can think of one other offbeat but definitely theistic possibility.

OSCAR: This ought to be good. Your offbeat theories can be pretty entertaining.

SOPHIE: Try this. When we think of an all-perfect God, we separate the concept of perfection into categories, such as omnipotence, omniscience, and omnibenevolence, right?

OSCAR: Yes. We went through that in that other dubious argument about God's being too perfect not to exist.

SOPHIE: You're a quick learner, Oscar. Well, maybe we need to change the way we look at perfection, as it might apply to God.

DAVID: A different way of thinking about perfection? I don't think I understand what you mean.

SOPHIE: I hope I can explain this. Imagine a universe with just God in it, sitting there alone. He's omnipotent, so he can create any kind of universe he chooses; but he's also omnibenevolent, so he doesn't want to create a universe that allows for unnecessary suffering. He's also omniscient, so he knows what he has to do to accomplish these things, but there's still a kind of knowledge that he can't possibly have.

DAVID: How can that be, if he's omniscient?

SOPHIE: He can't have finite experiential knowledge.

DAVID: What does that mean?

SOPHIE: He can't know what it is like to have a finite, time-bound perspective on reality. He can't know what it is like to suffer and grow. That's what I mean by *experiential* knowledge. To know what something is like, you must have experiences of a certain sort. If God is an infinite and eternal being, he is just not the right sort of being to have finite and time-bound knowledge.

DAVID: But is that an imperfection, not to be able to see the world only partially and flawed, the way we see it?

SOPHIE: Instead of thinking of it as an imperfection, think of it as simply a kind of knowledge that could exist in some universe, but not in a universe that contains *only* an infinite and eternal being.

OSCAR: So what's the problem? All this being has to do is step out of eternity and into time for a while, to mask off some of his infinite vision and take a finite look at things.

SOPHIE: At *what* things? You've hit the nail on the head though, Oscar. To realize genuine omniscience, God must figure out a way to step out of infinity and eternity into finitude and time. My idea is that the way he chose to do this was to create a universe populated with finite beings who are somehow evolving toward perfection.

OSCAR: But how does that help God to gain finite experiential knowledge?

SOPHIE: That's the beauty of it. We mortals *are* his finite peepholes into the universe of time. Our experience becomes his experience, including the suffering. You see, this is the continuation of my "argument from consciousness" which you found so weird.

DAVID: That's a very powerful image, Sophie. But doesn't it make it seem that we are being *exploited* by a voyeuristic God?

SOPHIE: It would be like that if our lives ended at death. But if we are somehow evolving toward perfection ourselves, then we also reap all the rewards of this evolutionary work. That is the payment for the suffering. This theory not only explains the suffering, but also says something about why God would create a universe with creatures like us in it at all.

OSCAR: Your theory has a certain appeal, but it is all pretty speculative.

SOPHIE: I admit that. But here's my way of thinking about it: If *I* were in charge of this universe, how would I arrange things? I agree with David that I wouldn't want a universe that lacked opportunities for moral growth, and I wouldn't have the process of growth end at death. Instead, I'd set it up so that learning and growing would continue indefinitely, so that in the fullness of time we would all reach higher and higher levels of wisdom. This way, our mortal existence could be the first step of a long climb away from ignorance and suffering, toward God.

OSCAR: Are you talking about reincarnation or some such thing?

SOPHIE: Not specifically. There are lots of different possible ways of thinking about this evolutionary process. The point is that instead of thinking of suffering as a "payment" for bliss in the next world, I see it as the start of a long path toward learning and growth. You know, even as children we humans have our share of fear and pain. We three are not that old, but we're old enough to recognize that the fears and pains of childhood are part of what got us to where we are now. And in twenty years we'll be saying similar things about these years. So yes, some lives are cut short or made horrible by disease and other misfortunes. And it's doubtful that those people's suffering does much to uplift the rest of us. But if the people themselves continue to experience suffering and are uplifted by it, then that suffering is not a "payment" for anything but a *contribution* to something. That's how I would arrange things.

OSCAR: But you're not God.

SOPHIE: No, but if I'm going to think about God, I might as well think with the highest ideals that I can imagine. I can even believe that the fact that I have those ideals is itself a kind of "overendowment," a subtle sign that my thinking is being pulled in a direction that points to something beyond the observable world of suffering and death.

DAVID: That's certainly not a traditional view, Sophie, but it does make a certain amount of sense, especially the part about not viewing suffering as "payment" for an eternal "reward." I'd have to give this one a lot of thought.

SOPHIE: There's all the time in the world for that, David.

Chapter 6

Miracles

Later that day they meet in the main quadrangle of the campus. Oscar is bemoaning his prospects for passing a math exam that is scheduled for the next week.

OSCAR: It's just too much material to cover on a single exam, and it's all about proofs and formula derivations. The prof says we're supposed to be able to reproduce the key parts of the proofs for all the main theorems of the course. It'll take a miracle just for me to remember what the theorems are.

DAVID: It's just what they always say: Sooner or later, even the atheist finds himself in enough trouble that he prays for a miracle.

OSCAR: Don't start, David. It's a figure of speech, meaning that the task is *impossible,* just as miracles are impossible.

DAVID: They are? I guess I shouldn't be surprised to hear you say that. I've avoided mentioning miracles in our discussions about God, since I didn't suppose there would be any way to get you to take the idea seriously.

OSCAR: That shows sound judgment, David. There's no point wasting our time talking about impossible events as evidence for an impossible being.

SOPHIE: Wait, Oscar. I'm not sure I understand why you say that miracles are impossible.

OSCAR: What's to understand? "Impossible" isn't such a difficult concept, is it?

SOPHIE: It can be a bit slippery. Do you mean that miracles are inconceivable?

OSCAR: What do you mean by "inconceivable"?

SOPHIE: To say that something is inconceivable is to say that the idea itself makes no sense, like a four-sided triangle. Inconceivable means *logically* impossible.

OSCAR: I see. I guess that's not what I mean. I can conceive of what might count as a miracle, but I know that that sort of thing is impossible.

DAVID: Just for the record, Oscar, what sort of thing do you have in mind as something that would count as a miracle?

OSCAR: You know, something *miraculous!* Suppose you were to float slowly up in the air right in front of me, David, and hover there for a minute or so. That would be a miracle.

DAVID: Sounds more like magic to me.

OSCAR: Exactly. There's no difference. Both are impossible.

SOPHIE: What makes you say that that would be impossible, Oscar?

OSCAR: Have you ever seen anyone levitate, Sophie?

SOPHIE: Can't say that I have, but so what? Am I supposed to believe that things are impossible unless I've seen them happen?

OSCAR: Of course not. The point is that you're not *about* to see anyone levitate, either. In fact, David made this very point today when he said that the laws of nature are the boundary between what is possible and what isn't. Levitation is a violation of physical law, and that's what makes it impossible.

DAVID: I was talking about what is possible in the normal course of things, within the so-called natural order. I wasn't trying to say that there are no miracles.

OSCAR: You may not have been trying to say it, but you did say it.

SOPHIE: So let me get this straight, Oscar. You're saying that miracles are impossible *because* they are violations of physical law. Is that it?

OSCAR: Yes, that's exactly right.

SOPHIE: Maybe we need to clarify what we mean by "miracle" in this discussion.

OSCAR: A miracle would be an extraordinary event, such as levitation, or returning from the dead.

SOPHIE: I don't think "extraordinary event" is definite enough. Take this for example: The other night I was listening to the radio and I heard an interview with a man who writes books about the influence of the mind on physical health. I knew that my cousin was very much interested in this sort of thing, so I wanted to call her and tell her who this man was, and the name of his book. But she lives about fifteen hundred miles away, and I couldn't find her number anywhere. Just as I was about to give up in disgust, the phone rang and it was my cousin. I thought that was a pretty extraordinary event. Do you think it was a miracle?

DAVID: I think that something like that *could* be a miracle, because it could show God's involvement in human affairs.

OSCAR: Well, I don't consider that sort of thing a miracle at all. It's a coincidence and nothing more.

SOPHIE: But it is an extraordinary kind of event, isn't it? It's not the way things ordinarily work—to be called by the person whose number you are trying to find. So if that wasn't a miracle, then you're going to have to narrow down your definition. If miracles are extraordinary events, in what way are they extraordinary?

OSCAR: They have to be extraordinary in a more fundamental way; they have to violate the laws of nature.

SOPHIE: So that's what you meant when you said that levitation would be a miracle *because* it violates physical laws. It's a miracle according to your definition.

OSCAR: Right.

SOPHIE: What are these laws of nature that you are talking about, and how do we know about them?

OSCAR: What are they? I thought we'd already been through that. The laws of nature are the basic rules about how things happen in nature. We know about them by having made careful observations over long periods of time.

SOPHIE: Do the laws of nature describe how things *must* happen, or merely how they *do* happen?

OSCAR: I don't understand what you're asking. If the laws of nature say that things happen in a certain way, then that's the way they have to happen, in this universe at least.

SOPHIE: It seems to me that what you are saying is this: Scientists have spent much time and effort carefully observing the regularities in natural processes. Some of these observed regularities are so well confirmed that we call them laws of nature, but they are still observed regularities.

OSCAR: Okay, I'm willing to go along with that. Laws of nature are observed regularities, so well confirmed that they are exceptionless.

SOPHIE: To say that levitation is a violation of physical law, then, is to say that levitation is never observed to happen.

OSCAR: Right. It can't happen because it violates the laws of nature.

SOPHIE: No, no, you're adding something extra to this. To say that levitation violates the laws of nature is to say that levitation is never observed to occur. To say that something *doesn't* happen is one thing; to say that it *can't* happen is something else.

OSCAR: No it isn't, not at the level of the laws of nature. If David started levitating right now, I'd have to say that certain things that we thought are laws of nature really aren't, because levitation is incompatible with the world described by those laws. The laws would have to be abandoned or changed.

SOPHIE: Ah, but now you've made it logically impossible for the laws of nature to be violated. You're saying that if something appears to violate them, then they aren't really the laws of nature. That means that a so-called miracle isn't a violation of the laws of nature but rather is proof that the recognized laws of nature are false.

DAVID: This reminds me of something St. Augustine said: "Miracles are not violations of nature's laws, but only of what we know of nature's laws."

SOPHIE: Is that what you are saying, Oscar? If so, it means that laws of nature cannot even be conceived to be violated.

OSCAR: All right, all right. I'm not sure. This seems like a verbal quibble to me. What does it really have to do with whether miracles happen?

SOPHIE: We want to be as clear as possible about what the issues are. If there is a phenomenon that does not fit with what we understand the laws of nature to be, do we conclude that it is a miracle?

OSCAR: I suppose we don't. More likely, it means that we have to either modify the laws or discover the new ones that govern the phenomenon. I'm thinking of the way irregularities in the observed orbit of Mercury led to changes in the "law" that light always moves in a straight line through space. Mercury's orbit wasn't *miraculous;* it was just anomalous, until Einstein figured it out.

SOPHIE: Right. The orbit of Mercury, although it didn't fit the traditional laws, conformed to a different set of laws, which scientists were able to discover. It was "irregular" with respect to the traditional laws, but it had a regularity of its own. It was still "lawlike" in its behavior. I think a miracle would look somewhat different. My idea is that although a miracle would not fit the known laws of nature, neither would it appear to be lawlike at all.

DAVID: What do you mean by that?

SOPHIE: I mean that it is of the essence of miracles that they are not *predictable*. Mercury may have violated what we thought was a physical law, but it did so predictably, so there was every reason to think that we would eventually be able to show that it did conform to some physical law or other. Now we know that light is bent in the vicinity of gravitational fields, so we have "fixed" the law that Mercury's orbit was sometimes breaking. Now let's think about levitation again. Suppose David were to levitate, but only when he ate almonds; otherwise, he would remain gravity-bound like the rest of us.

OSCAR: What would that show?

SOPHIE: Even though it is inexplicable that David should levitate while eating almonds, the fact that it is a dependable and predictable phenomenon would suggest that there is some weird physical law at work. Extraordinary as that would be, I wouldn't call it a miracle. If he just levitated *once*, or at random intervals, that would be more miraculous.

DAVID: Wait a minute, Sophie. I see what you're getting at, and I agree up to a point; but I think you're missing something. Miracles may be unpredictable, but I don't think they are mere random events.

OSCAR: If you can't predict them, how could they be anything *but* random?

DAVID: I think that both of you have been so focused on the violation-of-physical-law aspect of miracles that you have overlooked the other part, which is far more important. Miracles are meaningful occurrences. They are signs of God's intervention in the events of nature.

OSCAR: But that's begging the question, if you're going to use miracles as evidence of God, which is what I thought was the whole point of this discussion.

SOPHIE: No, David's right. Obviously, we can't simply presuppose that miracles are acts of God, but we can say that they are the sorts of things that would make sense as acts of God. They ought to appear meaningful, even though they are not predictable or repeatable. An apparently pointless nonrepeatable violation of physical law would not be a good candidate for a miracle.

OSCAR: How do we know what's pointless and what isn't?

SOPHIE: We don't, at least not all the time. The point is not to have an infallible criterion. What we have is a criterion that ought to enable us to recognize at least some miracles, even if we also fail to recognize some.

OSCAR: So what sort of things are we talking about? Water into wine?

DAVID: There are many instances of miracles in the Bible, as you well know, but I doubt that you would accept them as such. Maybe it would be more to the point to consider miraculous cures of physical illness, like the things that sometimes happen at Lourdes.

OSCAR: You mean people throwing away their crutches and saying "Thank you, Jesus"? Is that the best you can do?

DAVID: It doesn't really sound like you've looked into this sort of thing very deeply. The Catholic Church maintains an office at Lourdes whose purpose is to authenticate claims of miracle cures. They require certified medical histories and confirmations of cures. They end up rejecting many claims, meaning not that the claims are phony but that they can't be authenticated. But many *can* be.

OSCAR: No doubt. Even I wouldn't say that all of them are deliberate frauds. It seems to me, however, that a better explanation is that the human body has powers to heal itself that we don't yet fully understand. It could be some form of psychosomatic effect. God doesn't need to be involved at all.

DAVID: That sounds like an easy way out, Oscar. "Unknown healing powers" doesn't tell me very much.

OSCAR: And "miraculous" doesn't tell me very much. All that I'm saying is that we do know that psychosomatic effects are real, and they can be very dramatic. It doesn't seem like too much of a leap to suppose that what appear to be miracle cures will eventually be explained along those lines.

SOPHIE: I can't help thinking, Oscar, that you are using terms like "psychosomatic effects" in a way that may be ignoring some important assumptions.

OSCAR: Psychosomatic effects have been recognized for a very long time, so it's not as though I'm concocting some new category of phenomena to bolster my argument. I just think that the sorts of so-called miraculous cures that David is talking about are more likely to be instances of psychosomatic effects.

SOPHIE: I understand. But how much do we really know about psychosomatic effects?

OSCAR: I'm sure there's plenty that we don't understand about them, but what's your point? Do we have to have a complete understanding before I can suggest them as an alternative to *miraculous* effects?

SOPHIE: I'm saying that psychosomatic effects are no less puzzling than miracles. There's an awful lot about the healing process that we don't understand; it gives only an illusion of understanding to apply the scientific-sounding label "psychosomatic."

OSCAR: Fair enough. But the same can be said about miracle healing. If the healing process is so poorly understood—and I won't argue with that—then we are not in a very strong position to say that a given case is miraculous, are we?

DAVID: Maybe not, Oscar, but I think the evidence is impressive, just the same.

OSCAR: Let's just say that *something* very interesting and powerful is going on in these cases and leave it at that. It's too much of a leap from there to the conclusion that they are acts of God. What other miracles do you have up your sleeve?

DAVID: Since we were talking about levitation before, I was thinking of the case of St. Joseph of Copertino, whose levitating was witnessed by many people.

OSCAR: Oh, really? When was this? I would have thought everyone would know about it.

DAVID: It was in the seventeenth century. They say that he would sometimes spontaneously levitate during mass, to the point that his monastery brothers would lock him in his cell to prevent the disruption that the levitation would cause. He was observed by numerous people, including skeptics.

OSCAR: I'm sure. Did any of this take place under controlled conditions? I doubt it. What you're telling me boils down to this: There exists some testimony to the effect that this St. Joseph levitated. I've never doubted the existence of *testimony* to miracles. But why should I believe any of it?

DAVID: Why shouldn't you? It doesn't take a trained observer to recognize levitation. You'd know it if you saw it, wouldn't you?

OSCAR: Yes, but I'd want to perform tests to make certain of what I was seeing. I'd want to make it as objective as possible.

DAVID: What makes you think these witnesses *weren't* objective?

OSCAR: Well, this was three hundred years ago and—

SOPHIE: Just a minute, Oscar. I am suspicious of an argument that rests on the premise that people of earlier times were inherently less objective and more gullible than contemporary people. I don't know the particulars of this case, but it seems bigoted to doubt it because people in the seventeenth century reported it.

OSCAR: Are you telling me you *believe* this story, Sophie? I'm just pointing out that this was at the beginning of modern science. Scientific method was not widely appreciated, especially in monasteries!

SOPHIE: I think there's plenty of room for doubt about that. But are you saying that one must be a scientist to be a credible witness of levitation?

OSCAR: The point is that for something as incompatible with physical law as levitation, a very high level of evidence is called for.

DAVID: In other words, you raise your standards of evidence for things that don't fit into your understanding of the way things are. No offense, but that doesn't sound like a particularly open-minded way of looking at the question. A while ago you said that violations of the laws of nature are *never* observed to happen. Now when I tell you that they have been observed to happen, you complain that the observations weren't valid.

SOPHIE: Whether he knows it or not, Oscar is using David Hume's argument about miracles. Hume stated that miracles are, by definition, violations of our best-confirmed generalizations about nature, which we sometimes call "laws." Where the evidence for a miracle is testimony, we have to ask what is more likely, that the testimony is mistaken or that those generalizations are wrong. We would have to conclude that it's always more likely that the testimony is mistaken. "Extraordinary claims require extraordinary evidence."

OSCAR: Exactly. I think Hume was right on the money. There's nothing bigoted about it; it's just the way knowledge works.

DAVID: As a general rule of thumb I don't have a problem with it. I just don't think it is reasonable to use this principle to insist upon *impossible* levels of evidence for miracles, just because they are thought to be impossible. I agree that levitation is an extraordinary claim to substantiate. But the testimony of multiple witnesses, on different occasions, under different conditions, is extraordinary evidence.

OSCAR: Not to me. The eyes can play strange tricks, and so can the mind. Too bad the episode wasn't videotaped.

DAVID: I can't believe you'd brush this off because it wasn't videotaped in the seventeenth century!

OSCAR: I'm not *blaming* anyone for not being able to produce proper evidence. Under the prevailing conditions, it may just not have been possible to do so.

DAVID: You know, I think that even if someone videotaped levitation tomorrow you'd claim that the tape was faked.

OSCAR: Probably. After all, what's more likely, that the tape was faked or that someone levitated? I'd want to know who made the videotape and how trustworthy that person is.

SOPHIE: It's interesting that it comes back to the trustworthiness of persons again, Oscar. You don't trust the seventeenth-century witnesses, and you wouldn't trust a twentieth-century videotape unless you could verify the trustworthiness of the people who made it. But to do that you'd have to rely on the testimony of still other people about their trustworthiness. You'd have to have a statement like, "I, Jan Doe, do swear that Jim Smith, who made this videotape of levitation, is a thoroughly honest person and a relentless skeptic who would never produce a fake." And of course you would need to know something about Jan Doe, who is doing the swearing. Ideally, you would want to know Jim Smith yourself, right?

OSCAR: Ideally, yes. Better yet, I'd like to *be* Jim Smith, to have made the videotape myself.

SOPHIE: That means that your ultimate measure of extraordinary objective evidence is utterly subjective: your instinctive trust in your own private judgment. Isn't this the very *opposite* of scientific method?

OSCAR: Not at all. It's the essence of scientific method that evidence is presented by a member of a community of scientists who trust one another's integrity. Without that, the whole thing would crumble.

SOPHIE: That's fine, but don't lose sight of the fact that one of the ways that community remains intact is by deciding not to trust those whose findings don't fit in.

OSCAR: Right. And that's as it should be. If those findings have merit, they will eventually be recognized by more and more people, and they will make it into the domain of accepted scientific knowledge. There are lots of examples of this; one is continental drift.

SOPHIE: Fair enough. But it does seem that with miracles, by their very anomalous nature, there will always be grounds for suspicion, and therefore they will never be scientifically validated, even if they are as real as rain. To put it another way, scientific method just isn't set up to accommodate nonrepeatable phenomena. If there are such things, they won't be a part of science, so it's not reasonable to say that they are *not* real *because* they're not scientifically validated.

DAVID: I never thought of it that way, Sophie. It's as if miracles are stuck in a Catch-22 category.

OSCAR: You may be right, Sophie, but that still leaves us with the result that miracles cannot prove God's existence.

SOPHIE: Maybe not, Oscar. Nevertheless, for people who already have a belief in God, miracles can confirm it. Even though they cannot refute the skeptic's beliefs, they can support those of the faithful.

OSCAR: I'm not so sure about that. Either something is evidence or it isn't. It shouldn't matter what you are already inclined to believe. That's what objectivity is about.

DAVID: But you already got rid of that when you said that unbelievable claims need more evidence. That means that evidence *does* depend on what you are already inclined to believe.

OSCAR: I still don't see how we can get around the point that we should have good reasons for what we believe. Proper evidence ought to incline *anyone* to believe.

DAVID: You know, Oscar, I sometimes get the impression that you think that if people were really rational, they would just look at the evidence and agree about everything.

Oscar: I wouldn't put it that way, David. Rational people can disagree about things because they are in possession of different information, or because they are not equally capable of appreciating the evidence. But I do think that, in principle, the proper use of reason ought to tend to decrease the disagreements between people. But that's an ideal. No one is perfectly rational—except me—and no one has *all* the information.

Sophie: Maybe we need to talk about how certain kinds of experiences are more basic to our worldview than what we can or can't produce "proper evidence" for.

Oscar: I don't think I know what you mean, but I'm always willing to hear more.

David: Me too, but not right now. I've got a load of work to do. Maybe we can get together tonight sometime and pick it up again. I think this is the part that has more to do with why people actually believe in God than do any of the so-called proofs. Why don't we meet in the coffee shop around 9:30?

Chapter 7

Experience as Knowledge

They have met in the coffee shop, all of them rather tired. Oscar sits with his head thrown back, eyes closed. Sophie is sketching something on a pad. David, carrying coffees back to the table, is eager to resume the discussion.

DAVID: Here you are, folks. This coffee has been sitting there awhile; it ought to be good and strong.

OSCAR: Will it make me see God?

SOPHIE: Let us know if it does, will you? So where did we leave off this afternoon? It seems as if it was two weeks ago.

DAVID: Sophie, you had suggested that people have experiences that make the whole project of producing proof of the existence of God irrelevant. At least, that's what I thought you were getting at.

OSCAR: Oh yeah, that's right, Sophie. What was that all about?

SOPHIE: I wasn't thinking about making the proofs for the existence of God irrelevant, but it does seem to me that one reason why rational people disagree about things like God is that they have had different kinds of experiences in their lives. I am thinking about the whole phenomenon called "religious experience," and how important it is. For many people, this is what belief in God is all—

OSCAR: Hold it. Before you start gushing, could you tell me what this religious experience is supposed to be? I mean, are we talking here about visions and voices?

SOPHIE: We could be. At one end of the spectrum there are the intense mystical experiences, but there are other kinds, too.

DAVID: That's right. For some people it's a dramatic, sudden, and visionary thing. The classic case is St. Paul's experience on the road to Damascus. There are stories like that in all the religions of the world.

OSCAR: And what's at the other end of the spectrum? Sneezing?

SOPHIE: Very clever, Oscar. For some people, it seems to be a feeling of presence, a sense of being looked after. For others, it's like a shift, a different way of thinking. It's hard to describe—

DAVID: A "shift" is a good way to put it, Sophie. It's like a reordering of thought processes. It's not that you see anything new or different, but what you do see and experience takes on a different meaning. This is how it was for me, anyway. It is hard to describe, but it's as if things that seemed like accidents one day begin to seem like parts of a plan the next day. My life seemed less and less like a series of random events for me to navigate through, and more like a story with a point. And it's a self-confirming thing: The more I look for confirmation that my life is unfolding according to a plan, the more it seems to happen that way. The more I trust the idea that things happen for a reason, the more reason I can find in them.

OSCAR: What does this have to do with God?

DAVID: Once I began to experience my life as working out according to a plan, I felt that I was in some sort of relationship with a planner. It's something like that feeling of presence that Sophie mentioned.

OSCAR: That's it?

SOPHIE: You have to understand, Oscar, that religious experience is notoriously difficult to express verbally, especially to someone who doesn't relate personally to the idea.

OSCAR: That's very convenient. But look, I don't doubt that people have the kinds of experiences you are describing. I just don't see any reason to take them as experiences of God.

SOPHIE: Why don't we talk about mystical experiences first, since they are particularly dramatic?

OSCAR: Fine. The more dramatic, the better.

SOPHIE: Well, if you look at the mystical literature of the world's religions, you'll find many descriptions of people having "peak experiences," which they describe in various ways as "union" or "communion" with God, depending on the particular theology within which they are working. They claim to achieve a state compared to which ordinary day-to-day consciousness seems almost dreamlike. Sometimes these experiences are spontaneous, and sometimes they are the result of disciplined cultivation, as in yoga or contemplative prayer.

OSCAR: And sometimes people have such experiences after taking drugs. That suggests to me that what these people are really experiencing here is the result of some unusual changes in their brain chemistry, possibly as a result of these weird "disciplines" that you mentioned. Again, it's not a matter of doubting that people have these mystical experiences; but if we can get pretty much the same experience by swallowing LSD, or whatever, then it's hard to believe that this is an experience of God, as opposed to altered brain chemistry.

DAVID: I have to admit, Sophie, that I've often thought much the same thing about the mystical experiences. The fact that they can be drug-induced does seem to undermine them as valid experiences of God.

SOPHIE: But you both are assuming that if a certain kind of experience can be triggered, in some form, by a chemical, then it has no other meaning. You talk about experience of God *as opposed* to altered brain chemistry. There are alternatives to this oppositional way of thinking. If you assume at the start that all mental states are nothing more than events in the brain, then of course mystical experiences are no different. But if you take seriously the possibility that there's more to *all* experience than brain chemistry, then it's also possible that things that happen in the brain might actually expand what we are capable of knowing.

DAVID: How is that possible? Can you give an example of what you are talking about?

SOPHIE: Think of mathematics and such mathematical truths as that the square root of two can't be expressed as a fraction. It's pretty clear that human beings can understand this truth, and dogs can't. It's also clear that this is because of differences in the brain structure of humans and dogs. If dogs could somehow get into the right brain state, they'd be able to understand it, too. But we shouldn't conclude from this that the fact that the square root of two is irrational is just a product of brain structures. Having a bigger and more complex brain puts us in touch with "higher realities" than what a dog knows about.

Oscar: It's one thing to talk about two completely different types of brains being able to know about different things, and quite another to talk about two brains of the same type, one of which has some extra chemicals in it.

Sophie: Is it so different? In both cases, we're talking about changing the range of available brain states and getting, as a result of that change, different kinds of knowledge. For that matter, think of what a trained mathematician knows, most of which is far beyond my ability. There are entire branches of mathematics that I don't have a clue about. It's not so different from the mystic who after years of training and discipline achieves a kind of knowledge that the rest of us just don't get.

Oscar: But the "higher" mathematics is still basically just an extension of the "lower" mathematics that you do understand. The mystic wants us to believe that he or she has a completely different kind of knowledge, something fundamentally discontinuous with everything else we know. Plus, if I really want to know whether higher mathematics is meaningful, I can always learn it for myself.

Sophie: You can also take up the practice of mystical discipline, if you want to have the kinds of experiences that the mystics have.

Oscar: There's no guarantee that I'll succeed, though.

Sophie: There's no guarantee that you'll succeed with higher mathematics, either. The best we can say is that there is a substantial body of records suggesting that at least some people do succeed, and what's especially interesting is that this literature extends across cultural and historical boundaries. The Buddhist and Hindu mystics sound a lot like the Muslim and Christian mystics.

Oscar: And the drug users?

Sophie: Maybe. In some of the shamanic traditions, the use of psychotropic substances is seen as a valid form of initiation, a sort of preview of mystical knowledge, if not a completely reliable and safe way to become stabilized in it. Don't forget that religious mysticism is not just about having flashy experiences, but also about integrating those experiences into one's life. For our purposes, though, I think that the universality and robustness of mysticism give us some reason to believe that the mystics are onto something real.

OSCAR: But is it God?

SOPHIE: There is a problem of interpretation here, absolutely. Even though the mystics' descriptions of their experiences sound similar, there is a vast difference in the symbolism used to interpret them, and it is admittedly not easy to say where the experiences leave off and the interpretation begins. Buddhists don't interpret their experiences theistically; Jews, Christians, and Muslims do.

OSCAR: Then it really doesn't seem to amount to much support for the hypothesis that God exists, if some mystics don't believe in God.

SOPHIE: That's true, Oscar, if you insist on setting up a belief in God in opposition to other kinds of basic spiritual beliefs. I know there's a long tradition of that kind of opposition, but I see people like Thomas Merton as a sign that there are other options. He was a Trappist monk who *didn't* see any fundamental opposition between Christianity and Buddhism. And there have been others. The way I see it, these mystics are all experiencing a deep kind of connectedness to *something* that transcends what we usually take to be reality, and this connectedness has deep and life-changing effects. It's powerful, in some way that the rest of us find hard to understand. Once they begin to talk about their experience, however, they superimpose a symbolism on it, and the symbols that they choose will depend on what is most intelligible to them, which in turn depends a great deal on what they are used to. And so, it becomes God, or the Tao, or the Buddha-nature, or Shiva, or whatever. And as others try to systematize this material, it becomes theology.

OSCAR: It still sounds pretty thin to me. How many of us really have these kinds of experiences?

DAVID: Sophie made a good point, though, Oscar. You seem to be pretty keen on a materialistic, scientific worldview, but how many of us really know science at the level required to understand that worldview? In its fullness, the scientific worldview is just as inaccessible as the mystical worldview. What percentage of people understand, or are capable of understanding, something like, say, quantum electrodynamics? Very few, I'd say. But quantum electrodynamics is an important part of what the current scientific worldview is all about. Those of us who don't really "get it" are just going along with what others tell us to believe.

You said that higher mathematics is just an "extension" of basic mathematics. That may be true, but it is also misleading. Higher mathematics deals with things that are way beyond our ability to conceptualize in terms of everyday experience, like spaces with infinite numbers of dimensions. Mystics may be able to tune in to something that is as far beyond our usual experience as what the mathematicians and physicists study—I can't really say whether the analogy works because I'm not a mystic. For most of us, religious experience is less radical, even though it can still be very dramatic. That's why I prefer to think of religious experience in less mystical, more accessible terms.

OSCAR: Okay. Your idea is that people come to experience a sense of meaning and order in their lives, and less randomness. They feel that things happen for a reason; right?

DAVID: That's it. But the first step is to be open to experiencing life in this way, and I think that's what faith is all about. Two people could live through the very same experience; one would find it a more or less random thing, a chance occurrence generated by an indifferent universe, whereas the other would see meaning in it, lessons to be learned, reasons why it happened.

OSCAR: And what about the things that neither person can make any sense of?

DAVID: That's when the going gets tough, no mistake about it. At times like that—and I think every believer has to deal with them—it comes down to a matter of trust. The theist is likely to trust that the plan is nevertheless working, even if it is incomprehensible at that moment.

OSCAR: Nothing personal, David, but this thinking sounds childish to me, what the psychiatrists call "magical thinking." You go through your life believing in invisible causes and plans, things that you can't really figure out and certainly can't rely on. It just sounds very immature.

DAVID: I can understand your reaction, since it used to be my own stance. With people like Freud out there to argue that believing in God is an infantile projection of the father figure, it's easy to write the whole thing off. You know what changed my mind?

It was a teacher I had in high school, a physics teacher. This guy really impressed me with the power of his mind, his sense of humor, and his compassion. He really tried to help every student, and I found out that he was also involved in community service projects. He was a real role model for me, the kind of person I thought I wanted to be. He seemed the very opposite of infantile to me. It was only later that I found out that he had a deep and active belief in God; he never mentioned it in school. I was actually shocked to find this out, since I was full of views like yours about the childishness of religious belief. But I was honest enough to recognize that there was something wrong with my views. When I started to think about it, I found that I couldn't really justify the claim that believers are less mature than nonbelievers. On the contrary, when you go back in history, you find that many people of formidable intellect and great achievement have believed in God, not just childish and dysfunctional people.

OSCAR: But for most of history, belief in God has just been a part of people's background assumptions about reality. I suspect that many of these people believed in God simply because it was expected of them.

SOPHIE: Once again we arrive at the view that for most of history people were fogged in and incapable of critical thinking until we reached the vast sunlit spaces of the twentieth century. To listen to you, Oscar, one would think that atheism was just too difficult for, say, Pascal to figure out on his own. No, I think David has made a good point. If you are going to maintain that belief in God is a sign of some kind of mental immaturity, then you really need to show that believers as a group are less fully functional, mentally, than nonbelievers. You need to show that they have a problem of some sort. If you can't show that—and I really don't see how you could—then psychological buzzwords like "childish" and "magical thinking" don't really add any substance to the discussion.

OSCAR: But you both admit that mere religious experience doesn't add up to proof of God's existence, right?

DAVID: I admit it, sure. I only wanted to make the point that for many people, belief in God is about experience and not about proof.

SOPHIE: I think David's right. We've talked about lots of different arguments for the existence of God and seen that they are not conclusive. The atheist can find counterarguments, but to the person who has had a religious experience, the arguments tend to confirm the validity of that experience.

OSCAR: I think the theist ought to be able to do better than that, but we'll have to talk about it tomorrow. I'm too tired to keep going with this.

Chapter 8

Rationality without Proof

The next day, they meet outside the library, with some time to kill before lunch. After small talk about exams and papers, the conversation returns to where it left off.

DAVID: Sophie, a while ago you said you were going to say something about how a belief can be rational without proof. I think we've reached a point where we really need to talk about this.

OSCAR: I have a feeling that we are in for some spectacular philosophical stunt-flying. Sophie is about to show us how it's okay to believe in God, even though we've just finished trashing every argument put forward.

SOPHIE: Not so fast, Oscar. What we've done is to criticize all of the so-called proofs. But that is far from the end of the line.

OSCAR: But why should anyone accept something like the existence of God without proof?

SOPHIE: We need to talk again about what a proof is, and why we think it's so important to have one.

DAVID: I thought a proof is an argument where the conclusion follows from the premises. Is there more to it than that?

SOPHIE: It should be stronger than that. When you say that the conclusion "follows from" the premises, that means that it follows *necessarily* from the premises, so that if the premises are true, the conclusion cannot be false. But that's still not strong enough, since you could have a case where a conclusion follows necessarily from false premises, and that wouldn't be a proof. In a proof the premises really *are* true.

OSCAR: I don't see that this is getting us anywhere.

SOPHIE: Well, consider this: If the conclusion follows from the premises, then what do the premises follow from?

DAVID: That's easy. They follow from other premises.

OSCAR: I'm beginning to see the way the wind is blowing—

SOPHIE: Right. What do those other premises follow from? Some more premises; and they follow from . . . You see the problem? Where does the buck stop? We seem to end up with an infinite regress of premises, without any way to jump out of the system and decide whether they are all true or all false. If we want to avoid this infinite regress, it's clear that we have to make an important concession. If it's rational to believe anything at all *with* proof, then there must be some things which it is rational to believe *without* proof.

DAVID: I see. And the things which it is rational to believe without proof are the starting points for all of the other proofs.

OSCAR: Like Euclid's axioms.

SOPHIE: Yes, Oscar, *exactly* like Euclid's axioms. In order to prove anything at all, you need to accept some things without proof.

OSCAR: But who decides which things we are safe in accepting without proof? I hope you don't think you can now just jump in and posit the existence of God as an axiom. If you do, I'll posit the Easter bunny.

SOPHIE: Well, one criterion you could use is *self-evidence.* Euclid apparently felt that his axioms of geometry, such as "all right angles are equal," were simply self-evident. So, we could say that the only things which one is rationally entitled to believe without proof are self-evident things.

DAVID: That's fine, but self-evident to *whom?* Doesn't that end up being very subjective? I mean, what may be self-evident to one person could be ridiculous to someone else.

OSCAR: Couldn't have said it better myself.

SOPHIE: Some truths are self-evident because they are logically necessary, like the truth that no bachelors are married. You won't find any disagreement about that one. Nevertheless, I admit that the existence of God isn't in that category. What concerns me is that we seem to be heading straight toward skepticism. Next, you're both going to tell me that we can't believe anything without proof, and so we can't get any proofs off the ground. Let's try another tack on this. Consider the famous "other minds" problem. You guys both know what your own minds are like; you both know that you have an "inner life." But how do you know that I have any inner life at all? How do you know I'm not one of those zombies that we were talking about?

DAVID: Well, Sophie, you speak, you act, you argue—you do all the things that I do, so why shouldn't I conclude that you, like me, have a mind? That's all I really have to go on.

SOPHIE: Well, I agree that that is a rational thing for you to conclude, on the strength of the similarity between my behavior and your own. But what I'm trying to get at is this: You can't *prove* that I have an inner mental life like yours. No matter how convincing my behavior may be, you still could be mistaken. Isn't that so?

OSCAR: Sure, but the probability is so small that it's not really worth worrying about.

SOPHIE: But what does anybody really know about the probabilities in a case like this? What makes it *probable* that I have an inner mental life, apart from the reasonable assumption that I do? I think that in this context, probability is just a figure of speech. Now, let me ask a question. Is it *rational* for you to believe that I have a mind, an inner life more or less like your own?

DAVID: Sure. In fact, it seems irrational to doubt it.

OSCAR: Okay, I'll go along with you. What's the punch line?

SOPHIE: Well, what if someone said that their sense of God's presence in the world is in the same class as their sense that I have a mind? They can't prove it, but they can't really doubt it either.

OSCAR: That's a big jump, Sophie. At least we have your behavior to go on. We can say what gives us the vivid sense that you are a thinking being like the rest of us. What is God's behavior?

SOPHIE: Nature itself is God's behavior. This "other minds" approach is very similar, in essence, to the Argument from Design, except it isn't supposed to be a proof. This is the sort of theism put forward by thinkers like Einstein. The idea is that if you look intelligently and sensitively at nature, you see not the design but the Designer herself.

DAVID: Herself?

SOPHIE: Why not? I haven't wanted to get into the gender issue, so I haven't complained about the continual use of male pronouns in referring to God. But it doesn't hurt to throw in a reminder that there are other questions at issue besides existence.

OSCAR: Let's postpone the discussion of God's gender, shall we? It's pointless to worry about the pronouns if there's no good reason to think they refer to anything real. This "other minds" argument still sounds like a delusion to me. It sounds as though you're taking a loose analogy between human behavior and natural order and offering it as a proof.

SOPHIE: No, I've already said that it isn't a proof. It's an account of how it might be rational to believe in God without proof. The point is that it isn't any less rational than believing that I have a mind.

OSCAR: But it *is* less rational! It's rational for me to attribute a mind to you, because your behavior is like mine. It's not rational for me to attribute a mind to a tree, because its behavior isn't anything like mine. And I can *say* in what respects your behavior is relevantly similar, and the tree's isn't. But the universe just doesn't act like me, and I frankly don't see how it could. So rationality seems to demand that I deny that the universe itself has a mind.

DAVID: Well, Oscar, since you just offered, maybe you should tell us what the criteria are for deciding whether it's rational to attribute a mind to something.

OSCAR: One of the most important ones is language. The fact that you and Sophie use language, just as I do, is powerful evidence to me that you have a mind, just as I do.

DAVID: Does that mean that infants don't have minds?

OSCAR: That's a fallacy, and you know it, David. I don't deny that there might be other reasons to attribute minds to infants. For one thing they tend to *become* language users. And I also don't deny that there might be troublesome borderline cases for this or any other set of criteria. I'm simply saying that among normal functioning adults, language is an important criterion. The universe doesn't talk. Are you going to tell me that God is an infant, or an aphasic?

SOPHIE: That's an interesting point. It's often pointed out that mathematics is a language. In fact, it has been claimed that mathematics is the language "spoken" by nature. That is where Einstein's point is coming from. To a trained mind, the universe *does* talk. And surely it's not cheating to insist on a "trained mind." After all, you need a trained mind to recognize human noises as language. The only difference here is the universality of the training. It may simply be that the universe appears mute to most of us because we are in a sense illiterates.

OSCAR: Well, it's a funny thing that not all of the trained minds are getting the message, then. There are many physicists with as much mathematical sophistication as Einstein who don't buy this line. There appears to be more to it than training.

DAVID: There are other kinds of training, too. This is where the idea of religious experience comes in. In many Eastern religions, there is great emphasis on meditation as a way to train the mind and make it more sensitive. What it becomes more sensitive *to* is not always called "God," as I understand it. But it may be that they are all talking about the same thing.

OSCAR: So I should learn higher mathematics and take up meditation now?

SOPHIE: Well, I don't think either would hurt anybody. But David raises an interesting point. If one kind of religious belief is a kind of attunement to nature itself, it may be that what made Einstein unusual—unusual for a Western scientist, that is—was the particular kind of temperament with which he approached science and mathematics. And remember, a common theme in the religions of the world is that spirituality takes *work,* of some sort. The Buddhists, for example, say that even though everyone is enlightened, it takes effort to recognize one's own inherent enlightenment.

OSCAR: But I really think we've gotten away from the rationality of belief in God.

SOPHIE: In a way you're right, Oscar. At least we've gotten away from a narrow, strictly logical sense of rationality. But that only shows that the problem of rationality cannot be approached as in a vacuum; it shades off into other matters, such as sensitivity, attunement, openness, and so forth. It may well be that the belief in God, as it is typically understood by most Westerners, as an oversized anthropomorphic person who is "out there" somewhere *is* irrational. Or if it's not irrational, perhaps it is just too limited. Humankind's conception of the spiritual has had to change before; it's not unreasonable to expect that it will have to change again. I don't think Einstein, even though he was a Jew, believed literally in Yahweh, the God of the Old Testament. His conception was much more subtle and mystical and, perhaps, more mature and suitable for a scientific age. My own feeling—and it is just a feeling—is that if there is any truth at all to religious beliefs, then that truth must be common to *all* religious beliefs. I don't mean that I expect that all religions can somehow be brought into agreement with one another. I don't think that's possible, or even desirable. I mean that it ought to be possible to seek and find convergence at the level of the highest spiritual principles of all the religions.

OSCAR: Then that lets God out of the picture. The Buddhists don't believe in God.

SOPHIE: Does it? Or does it call for a reinterpretation of what we think we might mean by "God"? As I say, it wouldn't be the first time. It may turn out that the minimal concession to theism is the simple claim that there is something godlike about nature, or behind nature.

OSCAR: Even I could accept that, at least on alternate Tuesdays.

DAVID: Yes. But I have to admit that I find it disquieting to find so little direct support for the particular conception of God that I have been taught. On the other hand, I think that religious experience is what makes the idea of God "self-evident" as an axiom for at least some of us.

SOPHIE: There are no easy answers. I think that enough has been said to show that whatever its problems may be, theism cannot be dismissed offhand as irrational. The belief in God may take surprising forms, some of which we might not even be inclined to describe as "belief in God" but which nevertheless play the same role in a person's life.

OSCAR: Then let me ask one more question. You have argued persuasively that *some* sort of belief in God, *somehow* understood, is at least rational, if not provable. Is it irrational then to *disbelieve* in God?

SOPHIE: Of course not. It's quite rational to be an atheist, but the mode of rationality is different. You know, if one person believes one thing, and another person believes an exactly contradictory thing, logic tells us that they can't both be right. But logic does not tell us that they can't both be rational, since the rationality of a belief depends on a lot more than whether the thing believed is true or false. The fact of the matter is that rational people of good will disagree about things. That that fact isn't as obvious as it should be ought to provide a lesson in tolerance for all of us.

OSCAR: I don't know about this kind of tolerance. Either God exists or he doesn't. The theist and the atheist can't both be right, nor can they both be wrong.

SOPHIE: Sure, but that doesn't make either of them irrational. You're not saying that disagreement is irrational, are you?

OSCAR: Not exactly. When people disagree, it's usually because they have different information. They disagree about the *facts* of the case.

DAVID: What about the members of a jury? We should expect them to agree about the facts, since they are all presented with the same evidence and testimony. Yet jurors do sometimes disagree.

OSCAR: When people all have the same information and they still disagree, then it probably means that somebody is making a mistake in logic; that person is not connecting the facts to the right conclusion. When that happens, it ought to be possible to clarify the logic of the matter so that everyone agrees, and at that point the disagreement should disappear.

SOPHIE: That *is* the goal of the jury system, Oscar, and sometimes it works—but sometimes it doesn't.

OSCAR: Of course. Sometimes people refuse to see the facts or the logic that connects them, maybe because of some personal values that are at stake. I realize that this sort of thing happens, but it's still a kind of irrationality. And sometimes there just isn't enough information for the jury to reach a secure verdict, but they feel pressure to reach one anyway. In that case, the whole jury is acting irrationally, in my opinion.

SOPHIE: In real life, outside of jury boxes, nobody controls who gets exposed to what information. People have very different experiences. Not only that, they pay attention to very different sorts of things. They ask different questions and they listen to different kinds of answers. They have different ideas about what counts as a good reason for believing something.

OSCAR: They *shouldn't* have different ideas about what counts as a good reason for believing something. That's just a matter of logic, and reasoning is either sound or it isn't. It's not a matter of opinion.

SOPHIE: Oscar, I think you're idealizing the reasoning process. It might be possible to say exactly what counts as sound reasoning in a mathematical proof, but when you move away from formal reasoning, things just aren't so clear-cut. Consider the religious experiences that David was talking about. Your tendency is to minimize the importance of such experiences; for other people they are absolutely central to their experience of living. The difference is not just a matter of logic; it's a matter of what you choose to pay attention to in your life.

I agree with you that it's important to use logic carefully, and to try to identify premises that both parties to the discussion can agree on. It's important because when you do that you can avoid disagreements that arise from simple misunderstanding. To me, thinking carefully and honestly is what rationality is all about. But when the question is as subtle and complex as the existence of God, I can't pretend that any amount of carefulness and honesty will resolve all disagreements. Instead it will show what the disagreements are *really* about, and I think that usually turns out to be fundamental differences in how people interpret their own experiences. Disagreements of that sort are usually resolved not by arguments but by shared experience, compassion, trust, and things like that.

OSCAR: That still doesn't sound very rational to me. It sounds like you're saying that if we admire people, or feel sufficiently connected to them in some way, we tend to believe the things that those people believe. That may be true at a psychological level, but I can't accept it as a rational method that we should apply.

SOPHIE: But, Oscar, we all believe lots of things just because we have been told that they are true and we have decided that the people who told us are trustworthy. And what I'm talking about goes deeper than that. If you want to become an artist—a painter, say—the best thing you can do, after you learn the basics, is to spend as much time as possible in the company of artists whose level of achievement you trust. By doing that, you can gradually tune in to how they see the world; you notice what they notice, respond as they respond. Being an artist is not just having a set of beliefs, or even a set of skills; it's a way of life. It's the same in science. Sure, you have to learn a lot of information and skills, but eventually you have to hang out with scientists and learn how they think. I think this is also the way it works with religion and God. You don't just study philosophical theology; you connect with people whose lives are about God.

OSCAR: I should hang out with preachers?

DAVID: That's not what she means, Oscar. It's like what I was saying about my high school physics teacher. When you meet people like that, you can choose to open up to what is going on in their lives, or you can choose to disregard it. I think the logic and arguments can help to create a kind of opening for these experiences, but in the end you have to step out and trust something other than logic and arguments.

SOPHIE: I'm sure you don't think David has proven God's existence, and I bet you don't think you have disproved it, either.

OSCAR: No, but we agree that the burden of proof is on the theist.

SOPHIE: Fine, but we're looking beyond the proof issue now. We're looking at a kind of logically open space of possible beliefs, possible commitments, possible ways of life.

OSCAR: What are we supposed to do in this open space? Shouldn't we try to gather enough evidence to *close* it?

DAVID: That's one option, but there are others. Reason doesn't come to a screeching halt just because there's no absolute, decisive, conclusive proof. You know, this reminds me of "Pascal's wager" about belief in God. It's not another proof, so don't worry, but it is relevant to what we're talking about now. Have you heard of it, Oscar?

OSCAR: I don't think so. Was Pascal a betting man?

DAVID: He was a mathematician who had a profound religious experience, as a result of which he became a theist and a theologian. He had an interesting sort of meta-argument about belief in God.

OSCAR: A "meta-argument"? You're starting to sound like Sophie.

DAVID: The idea is that he didn't try to prove God's existence directly. Instead, he said that we should consider the consequences of belief and unbelief.

OSCAR: What consequences?

DAVID: Suppose that belief in God is necessary for salvation. If you believe in God, then, you have much to gain and very little to lose. If there is a possibility of immortality, for example, then the possible advantage of salvation is infinite compared to the minor and finite inconvenience that believing imposes on one's mortal lifestyle. So, if God exists, then if you believe in him, you win big; and if you don't, you lose much. If God doesn't exist, then if you believe in him you lose little; if you don't believe in him, you don't lose anything.

OSCAR: It seems to me that if I believed in God, I might be inclined to make some fairly major sacrifices in this life, though.

SOPHIE: Sure, Oscar, but even major sacrifices are trivial in comparison with the infinite benefits of immortality. Right, David?

DAVID: That's it. If you have everything to gain and little to lose by believing, then it makes sense to believe.

OSCAR: I'm not persuaded. For one thing, Pascal seems to think that I can just choose what to believe, despite the absence of any real evidence. The trouble is, God is simply not believable, at least for me.

SOPHIE: It's true enough that beliefs are not like switches that can be turned on and off, and I think Pascal understood that. His idea was that the belief in God can be cultivated, over time. It's what I was just describing, the process of connecting with people whose lives are about God, and tuning in to what they are doing and thinking.

• OSCAR: Maybe you could change your beliefs in that way; I don't think I could. I just don't see myself bothering to figure out what makes these people tick.

SOPHIE: But one of the things that we have seen again and again in this discussion is that the belief in God doesn't stand alone. It is linked to other beliefs and attitudes about reality. It's part of a whole orientation to the world. Your feeling that you could not budge from atheism is a measure of your commitment to a whole worldview, not just your conviction about a single belief.

OSCAR: I won't argue with that. I guess it's part of my worldview that, to be believable, the evidence for something like the existence of God must be more compelling than it is. Without more evidence, I am unwilling to cultivate the belief that would be my ante in Pascal's wager.

DAVID: This may be beside the point, but I've always had the feeling that God has good reason for not presenting us with *compelling* evidence of his existence.

OSCAR: You mean, he's not just being coy?

DAVID: Right. I think our *free assent* to God's existence is somehow important, maybe because it strengthens us in some way. It takes more determination and courage to believe in God than it does to believe in, say, the rings of Saturn.

OSCAR: So God wants us to stumble on him in the dark—is that it?

DAVID: No. I think he has arranged things so as to *attract* belief without *compelling* it. He makes his existence plausible, but he also gives us room for plausible denial, if that's what we want.

OSCAR: Why would he do that? If he wants us to believe, he could make his existence as obvious as the sun in the sky.

SOPHIE: Maybe a higher good is served by respecting our freedom not to believe. Maybe we should be glad that there is no proof that the theist can use to *force* the atheist to believe, or vice versa.

OSCAR: I don't know; I think God would want us to get it right.

DAVID: I think so too, Oscar, but I also think it might make a difference to him *how* we get it right. If logic and scientific method aren't enough to reveal the existence of God, then we have to make a choice: Either we try to understand and respect the religious experiences of people throughout the world and all of history, or we choose to minimize and dismiss those experiences. Maybe God wants us to have to make that choice.

SOPHIE: It could be as important to God that we learn to trust each other as it is that we trust the methods of logical argumentation.

OSCAR: Does that mean that I have to accept everything that anyone believes, no matter how bizarre or delusional?

SOPHIE: No, it doesn't. No one is suggesting that you throw away the tools of critical reasoning. But we have spent some time talking about arguments for God's existence. We haven't proved that he exists, but we have learned why the arguments are at least plausible to those who are inclined by their personal religious experience to believe in God. We also haven't shown that belief in God is bizarre or delusional. We come back to tolerance again. If God can give us space to form a rational belief in him without compulsion, maybe we can learn to do the same toward each other.

OSCAR: Amen to that.

Suggested Reading

A good place to start is with a general introduction to the philosophy of religion. John H. Hick's *Philosophy of Religion,* second edition (Englewood Cliffs, N.J.: Prentice Hall, 1973), for example, has a clear and concise presentation of Anselm's version of the Ontological Argument, which you will recognize as the "most perfect conceivable being" argument in Chapter 3. William Rowe's *Philosophy of Religion,* third edition (Belmont, Cal.: Wadsworth, 2001) is a very careful and balanced overview of the subject matter. Also useful is William J. Wainwright's *Philosophy of Religion* (Belmont, Cal.: Wadsworth, 1988), with good coverage of the First Cause argument and the problem of suffering. George Schlesinger's *Metaphysics: Methods and Problems* (Totowa, N.J.: Barnes & Noble, 1983) has a substantial and very clearly written section on the arguments for the existence of God, with an especially valuable discussion of the problem of suffering. His article, "The Problem of Evil and the Problem of Suffering," *American Philosophical Quarterly* 1 (1964), is very much worth reading. A very clear presentation of the "necessary being" argument, with attention to the Principle of Sufficient Reason, can be found in Richard Taylor's *Metaphysics,* fourth edition (Englewood Cliffs, N.J.: Prentice Hall, 1991).

More demanding surveys of the arguments can be found in such works as James Ross, *Philosophical Theology* (Indianapolis: Bobbs-Merrill, 1969), and Richard Swinburne, *The Existence of God* (Oxford: Oxford University Press, 1979). Ross offers an extensive treatment of the Ontological Argument, using modal logic; and Swinburne develops an interesting probabilistic argument for God's existence.

It's important to examine some of the classical sources, as well. Anselm's original presentation of the Ontological Argument is found in his *Proslogion*. An English translation is Thomas Williams's in *Monologion and Proslogion* (Indianapolis and Cambridge: Hackett Publishing Company, 1995). Possibly the most important historical contribution to the literature of arguments for the existence of God is the "five ways" of St. Thomas Aquinas, found in the *Summa Theologica*, Part I, Question 2. A good contemporary commentary on Aquinas's arguments is Anthony Kenny's *The Five Ways* (London: Routledge and Kegan Paul, 1969). The "natural order" argument, more commonly referred to as the Argument from Design, was given a vivid presentation in 1802 by William Paley, in *Natural Theology: or Evidences of the Existence and Attributes of the Deity Collected from the Appearances of Nature*. A recent abridgment of this is in William Paley, *Natural Theology: Selections* (Indianapolis: Bobbs-Merrill, 1963). The "garden" argument offered by David on page 31 is just a variation on Paley's "watchmaker" argument. An argument against the position that there is anything in evolution that suggests the work of an intelligent designer is *The Blind Watchmaker,* by Richard Dawkins (New York: Norton, 1987). Also, Oscar's comment on page 22 about how losing one's life is not really a loss comparable to losing a shoe is an informal statement of an argument put forward by the Greek philosopher Epicurus, and his later Roman disciple Lucretius, recorded in the latter's *De Rerum Natura*.

Religious experience is an intriguing subject, regardless of how one sees it in relation to the question of God's existence. A classic treatment is William James's *The Varieties of Religious Experience*. A recent contribution to the argument that religious experience does have value as evidence for the existence of God is *Perceiving God*, by William Alston (Ithaca, N.Y.: Cornell University Press, 1991).

Most of the above-mentioned works include, of course, discussion of criticisms of the various arguments for God's existence. There are, however, some entire books devoted to "atheology," or the refutation of the arguments for God's existence. One of the first and still very important such works was originally published in 1779: David Hume's *Dialogues Concerning Natural Religion* (Indianapolis: Hackett, 1980). Hume's argument against miracles, echoed by Oscar and cited by Sophie on page 68, appears in this work, as well as many other important challenges to theism. A more recent sustained attack on theism is J. L. Mackie's *The Miracle of Theism* (Oxford: Clarendon Press, 1982), in which

Mackie focuses on the arguments in Swinburne's *The Existence of God,* mentioned above. A useful anthology of essays in atheology is *The Varieties of Unbelief: from Epicurus to Sartre* (New York: Macmillan, 1989), edited by J.C.A. Gaskin.

The topic of miracles has its own literature. I have already mentioned Hume's attack in the *Dialogues.* A very readable defense of miracles is C. S. Lewis's *Miracles* (New York: Macmillan, 1947). Richard Swinburne's *The Concept of Miracle* (New York: St. Martin's Press, 1970) is also an important contribution. A very useful anthology, edited by Swinburne, is *Miracles* (New York: Macmillan, 1989). In case the mention of the levitation of St. Joseph of Copertino piqued your curiosity, you can read more about it and similar cases in Mircea Eliade, *Shamanism* (Princeton, N.J.: Princeton University Press, 1964). The case is also described in the fascinating book, *The Physical Phenomena of Mysticism,* by Herbert Thurston (London: Burns Oates, 1952).

The problem of evil/suffering also has a sizeable literature devoted to it. Hume's *Dialogues* are again an important source, from which Oscar's leading argument on page 48 is taken. The works by Swinburne, Schlesinger, and Mackie already mentioned also offer thorough discussions of this difficult topic. C. S. Lewis offers an eloquent theistic perspective in *The Problem of Pain* (New York: Macmillan, 1962). See also John H. Hick's *Evil and the God of Love* (New York: Harper & Row, 1966).

The "argument from consciousness" that Sophie presents in Chapter 4 and the linked argument on page 58 that God must "step out of infinity" to gain "experiential knowledge" are not part of the standard repertoire of arguments for God's existence. They are more speculative offerings, inspired by ideas that I have encountered in a number of sources, including *The Urantia Book* (Chicago: The Urantia Foundation, 1955); Nick Herbert's *Elemental Mind* (New York: Plume/Penguin, 1993); Paul Davies's *God and the New Physics* (New York: Simon & Schuster, 1983), and his more recent *The Mind of God* (New York: Simon & Schuster, 1992).

The problem of the tension between rationality and religious belief is very complex, overlapping onto more general questions about the nature of faith and rationality themselves. There are many interesting readings in this area, including Basil Mitchell, *The Justification of Religious Belief* (London: Macmillan, 1973); Gary Gutting, *Religious Belief and Religious Skepticism* (Notre Dame,

Ind.: University of Notre Dame Press, 1982); Ian Barbour, *Religion in an Age of Science* (San Francisco: HarperCollins, 1990); and Richard Swinburne, *Faith and Reason* (Oxford: Clarendon Press, 1983). The term "Pascal's wager," the discussion of which begins on page 89, is applied to sections 418 and 233 of Blaise Pascal's *Pensées,* which can be found in many editions of Pascal, including *Pascal: Selections,* edited by Richard H. Popkin (New York: Macmillan, 1989). A related reading, dealing with the question of whether beliefs can in fact be chosen, is William James's "The Will to Believe," found in many anthologies, including the collection of his writings entitled *The Will to Believe and Other Essays in Popular Philosophy* (New York: Dover, 1956). A different kind of contribution to the literature on faith and reason is *God and the Philosophers: The Reconciliation of Faith and Reason,* edited by Thomas V. Morris (Oxford: Oxford University Press, 1994), in which a number of contemporary theist philosophers describe how they have dealt with the tension between reason and faith in their own lives.